To the Rescue
A Passion for Pit Bulls

Connie Bowman

"Your book captured and kept my attention from beginning to end. It has all the elements a good book should have: it made me laugh; it made me cry; it made me aware of how cruel and inhumane, we as a society can be. Most of all, it lets the reader know that being a dog owner is a huge responsibility and anyone wanting to adopt or otherwise—a pit bull or any other breed dog for that matter—is a decision to be carefully considered.

"Your book left me wanting to read on. I didn't want it to end. My hope is that you will continue to write and share your experience and knowledge of being a dog/pit bull owner. Keep up the good work, and the good fight!"
                                                            Cami

To the Rescue
A Passion for Pit Bulls

Connie Bowman

Published by:

Joshua Tree Publishing
• Chicago •

www.JoshuaTreePublishing.com

All rights reserved. No part of this book may be reproduced or transmitted in any form or by any means, electronic or mechanical, including photocopying, recording or by any information storage and retrieval system without written permission from the author.

Copyright © 2014 Connie Bowman
ConnieToTheRescue.com

ISBN: 1941049109
13-Digit: 978-1-941049-10-5

Printed in the United States of America

Disclaimer:

This book is designed to provide information about the subject matter covered. The opinions expressed in this book are those of the author. Every effort has been made to make this book as complete and as accurate as possible. However, there may be mistakes both typographical and in content. Therefore, this text should be used only as a general guide and not as the ultimate source of information.

The author and publisher of this book shall have neither liability nor responsibility to any person or entity with respect to any loss or damage caused or alleged to be caused directly or indirectly by the information contained in this book.

DEDICATION

I dedicate my book to every pit bull/bully dog, past and present that like me, suffered by human hands. I am committed for the rest of my life to continue my fight to save you. If only one dog at a time...my motto is:

"One is better than none."

To my one and only, Anthony, for always understanding and not holding it against me when he should've came first.

To my husband John, the love of my life, for allowing me to do what I do and giving me the support that I needed.

To my sister Sonya, for encouraging me to write this book. And, to my sisters Sonya and Kathy, for always believing in me.

Contents

Dedication	3
I Am So Grateful...	6
Introduction	7
How Could You	9
To All The Dogs...	13
It Started with Frank	15
Cognac, a.k.a.	21
Pretty Boy Babe	21
Sonya To The Rescue	25
Serenity Breeze	31
Dogs Aren't the	35
Only Ones	35
Jesus Sent John My Way	41
Helen Ready	43
Trooper	47
More than One	51
The So-Called	55
No Kill Shelter	55
Two Great Danes	65
and a Spot	65
The Daily Juggle	71
The Inevitable	75
Looking Through Her Eyes	79
Damages	83

MY RESEARCH	87
NO MATTER WHAT	91
HOMECOMING	99
JOSEPHINA	103
LITTLE BITTY BUGGA BOO	107
LORD HAVE MERCY	113
WHY HAVE A DOG?	117
BOBO BOWMAN	123
PUMA	129
TENNIS SHOES	133
BUDDY	139
WALLY & PATRICK	143
OVER THE RAINBOW	153
THE RESCUER'S LAST REWARD	159
"YOU MADE ME"	163
IN HONOR OF...	164-165
CONNIETOTHERESCUE.COM	167

I Am So Grateful...

Thank You Jesus for being with me every step of the way. For giving me guidance and direction for my rescues. For carrying me through when I no longer had the strength. For keeping me in it when I thought I wanted out of it and making me persevere in helping your precious animals. For giving me the animals to love and most importantly…for their love in return.

Thank You Jesus for my husband and my family and close friends for all of their support and encouragement in writing this book and Thank You for my publisher, John Paul Owles, for believing in and publishing this book. I pray that you bless them and theirs always.

Thank You Jesus for loving me and allowing this to happen.

INTRODUCTION

This book has a collection of the individual stories about the pit bulls that I rescued over the years. They are my only passion in life.

I have always loved animals, and at a very young age, I experienced the physical and even worse, the emotional pain that people can inflict upon each other. But…animals never caused me pain. So, in my mind, I created my own little world, and in my world, there were animals and me. If I was hurting or sad or lonely, that's where I'd always go and always found comfort—that's where the animals rescued me. It was at that young age that I knew I wanted to give back to them what they so willingly gave to me, genuine unconditional love. For me, life without animals would be no life at all.

In 1993, I discovered a brand new love and a very deep passion for a particular breed of dog…the American Pit Bull Terrier.

My prayer in writing this book is to bring awareness and education. To not only open one's eyes but to open one's mind. To change the negative myths into the positive facts. If I can accomplish this, I'll know that I am fighting a good fight for my beloved Pit Bull Breed.

Rescue the weak and the needy;
deliver them from the hand of the wicked.
Psalm 82:3-4

How Could You

I am not the author of the following. It had been circulated around the rescue people and organizations and for some reason, I saved it. And now, it seems appropriate to share it some more.

" When I was a puppy, I entertained you with my antics and made you laugh. You called me your child—and despite a number of chewed shoes and a couple of torn up throw pillows—I became your best friend. Whenever I was bad, you'd shake your finger at me and ask, "How could you?" But, then you'd relent and roll me over for a belly rub. My housetraining took a little longer than expected, because you were terribly busy, but we worked on that together. I remember those nights of nuzzling you in bed, listening to your worries, and secret dreams. I believed that life could not be any more perfect. We went for long walks and runs in the park, rides in cars, stops for ice cream…and I always got the cone. And I took long naps in the sun waiting for you to come home at the end of the day.

Gradually, you began spending more time at work and on your career and searching for a human mate. I comforted you through heartbreaks and disappointments, never chided you about bad decisions. I waited for you patiently and romped with glee at your homecomings. Then you fell in love. She is now your wife but is not much of a dog person; yet still, I welcomed her into our home, tried to show her affection, and obeyed her. I was happy because you were happy.

Then the human babies came along, and I shared your excitement. I was fascinated by their softness and how they smelled…and I wanted to mother them, too. But the Mrs. worried that I might hurt them, so I spent most of my time banished to another room, isolated from the ones that I so loved.

As they began to grow, I became their friend. They clung to my fur and pulled themselves up on wobbly legs, poked fingers in my eyes, investigated my ears, and gave me kisses on my nose. I loved everything about them and their touch—for your touch was now no more. I would have defended them with my life if I had too. I would sneak into their beds and listen to their worries and secret dreams. Together we waited for the sound of your car in the driveway. There had been a time, when others asked you if you had a dog, that you produced a photo of me from your wallet and told stories about me. These past few years, you just answered "yes" and changed the subject. I had gone from being your dog to just a dog, one you now resented

Now you have a new career opportunity in another city, and you and they will be moving to an apartment that does not allow pets. You've made the right decision for your family, but there was a time when I was your family too. I was excited about the car ride until we arrived at the animal shelter. It smelled of dogs and cats, of fear, of despair. You filled out the paperwork and said, "Please find her a good home." They shrugged and gave you a pained look. They understand the realities facing a middle-aged dog or cat, even one with papers. You had to pry your son's fingers loose from my collar as he screamed, "No, Daddy, don't let them take my dog." And I worried for him, and what lessons you had just taught him about friendship and loyalty, about love and responsibility, and about respect for all life. You gave me a goodbye pat on the head. You avoided my eyes, and politely refused my collar. You had a deadline to meet, and now I have one too. After you left, the two nice ladies said you probably knew about your upcoming move months ago but made no attempt to find me another home. They shook their heads and said, "How could you?"

They are as attentive to us here in the shelter as their busy schedules allow. They feed us, of course, but I lost my appetite days ago. At first, whenever anyone passed by, I rushed to the front hoping it was you, that you had changed your mind…that this was all a bad dream. Or I hoped it would at least be someone who cared, someone who might save me. Then I realized you weren't coming back so I retreated to a far corner but still waited.

I heard her footsteps as she came for me at the end of the day, and I padded along the aisle after her to a separate room. A blissfully quiet room. She placed me on the table, rubbed my ears, and told me not to worry. My heart pounded in anticipation of what was to come, but there was also a sense of relief for I felt that my grief was killing me. As is my nature, I was more concerned about her. The burden which she bears weighs heavily on her. She gently placed a tourniquet around my foreleg as a tear ran down her cheek. I licked her hand in the same way I used to comfort you so many years ago. She expertly slid the needle into my vein.

As I felt the sting and the cool liquid coursing through my body, I lay down sleepily, looked into her kind eyes, and murmured, "How could you?" Perhaps, because she understood what she saw in my eyes, she said, "I am so sorry." She hugged me and explained to me that it was her job to make sure I went to a better place, where I wouldn't be ignored or abused or abandoned—or have to fend for myself. A place of love and light so very different from this earthly place.

With my last bit of energy, I tried to convey to her with a thump of my tail that my "How could you?" was not meant for her.

It was you, My Beloved Master.

I was thinking of, and I will still…wait for you forever."

~~ Unknown ~~

To All The Dogs...

That have died in shelters for no other reason than being born a bully breed, or spent their lives chained outside in the freezing cold or burning heat with only a barrel for shelter; that have been overbred and then thrown away; that have been fed ground up glass, hot peppers and gun powder to make you mean, if even fed at all; that have died fighting, all ripped apart and in agonizing pain; that have had their muzzles duct taped and used as bait to teach the others how to fight; that were thrown out of moving cars, thrown out of tall buildings, shot, stabbed, drowned, hung or set on fire and abandoned to die alone and in excruciating pain because you weren't tough enough; and, to those that are now being thrown into a car trunk with another to fight for your lives when only one survives only to be thrown back into a trunk with another to fight for your life once again…as long as I am on this earth with you, I will be fighting for you.

May God give us strength.

Chapter One

It Started with Frank

I had to go to school with my son, Anthony, to meet with his teacher. When we walked into the office, there was this not so cute, skinny little puppy. The staff was holding him for animal control to pick him up and take him to the pound—and this broke my heart.

Whenever I came upon an animal in some kind of need, in my mind, I always went back to my little animal world that I created when I was very young. I was reminded of how the animals always saved me and how I wanted to give back to them. So, I told the staff that I would take him home and try to find his owner—or find him a new home—and they agreed.

This little guy couldn't have been more than twelve weeks, and I couldn't imagine how he wound up at the school unless, somebody dumped him there.

When I picked up this little puppy, I realized he was in need of a bath so, the first thing I did was give him a bath. Then, I did all the typical things to do when a dog has been found: put an ad in the paper, check the lost ads, make some found flyers, etc. Back in

1993, we didn't have computers so there weren't a lot of options or resources for lost or found animals.

I'd take him on several walks everyday hoping somebody would see him and just have to have him. Two weeks went by, and this little puppy had wormed his way into my heart.

I didn't give him a name thinking that way I wouldn't get attached. But, now that he's worked his magic on me, I decided to name him "Frank."

I could tell that Frank was a mixed breed with Lab, and I don't know what. When I took him to the veterinarian, I asked him what he thought. "Pit Bull & Lab"

I had never heard of a pit bull before, but I wanted to know more. I read everything that had the words, "Pit Bull." Some things I read said pit bulls were vicious and were fighting dogs. I thought to myself that this cannot be true. All the dogs I have ever known were very sweet and loving. Besides, *who would want to fight their dogs*? This was beyond my comprehension. I chose not to believe in the negativity but, I must admit, that it stayed in the back of my mind. I saw pictures of strong, athletic beautiful dogs that came in all shapes, sizes and colors. I saw some of the same physical features in Frank—and I liked what I saw.

I truly believe that animals know when they have been rescued, and in so many different, kind ways, they show their appreciation.

Only Frank's way wasn't so kind. He was getting protective of me. If anybody got too close, he wouldn't hesitate to bite, or he'd stand his ground, look directly into your eyes, and growl as if he were saying, "Go ahead...make my day".

Although, I never encouraged him to protect me, I never discouraged him either. I actually liked the secure feeling I got, in fact I even thought it was cool the way Frank would, naturally protect me. I remember a time when my boyfriend and I got into an argument. My boyfriend had to throw a blanket over Frank, because Frank was coming at him.

He was very strong and quick to react. If anybody tried to pet him, he'd snap—and, if they'd reach over his head to pet him, he'd surely bite. I wondered if this behavior could be an indication that Frank had been abused and thought he was going to get hit.

He even bit my sister Sonya. She offered him a treat with one hand and reached over his head with the other hand. Frank bit her. Even drew blood. I'll never forget the devastation I saw in her face. She was so hurt but not from the bite. It was her feelings that hurt—and I hurt for her. Years later, she would say, "It is an honor if Frank Frank (as she called him) accepts you as his friend."

Apparently Frank doesn't like people and that was okay with me because I don't like people either. He did bite again, but this time, I was able to give fair warning to his victims. I told them he'll bite... they just didn't believe me. Frank had a mean streak in him. He'd watch your every move just waiting for the opportunity to bite; and when he did, he'd stand back with this funny look on his face like he was laughing at you.

I had fallen head over heels, madly in love with my dog Frank. I knew that I had my hands full and couldn't take any chances with him. I started thinking this isn't so cool anymore. Thankfully, nobody reported getting bit.

On the contrary, Frank had a carefully selected few that he did like. Surprisingly, but true. These were people that he chose to like and would never hurt, like Grandma.

I fell on hard times. Frank and I had to move to my mom and dad's mobile home park where we lived right across the street from their office/house. We'd see them coming and going throughout the day. Mom would go grocery shopping one day a week. I can't remember which day of the week, but Frank would surely know because on that day, around twelve or one in the afternoon, Frank would suddenly just stop whatever he was doing, go get his food bowl, and start heading over to Grandma's where she was carrying groceries into her house along with a bag of dog food that she always bought for Frank. He somehow knew it was grocery shopping day, and Grandma was coming home with food. Grandma was one of his selected few.

Frank had four different balls that were his favorite toys. We called them: the Tennis ball, the Bumpy ball, the Kong ball, and the Belly ball. I would tell Frank to go get his Kong ball; he'd sniff and search around, and within a few minutes, he'd find his Kong ball. Then I'd tell him to go get his Bumpy ball, and he did the same thing. I'd say, "Go get your Tennis ball" and he did. "Go get your Belly ball" and he got that one too. I didn't teach him to do this but Frank figured them all out.

Shortly after moving to Grandma's, we were able to move into our own apartment that allowed dogs. Whenever I was out walking Frank—and we saw another dog—I'd have to hold on for dear life because Frank would try to lunge at the other dog. This was very scary for me because there were many times I didn't think I could hold him back any longer. I could understand not liking people, but I couldn't understand not liking other dogs. I had never had a dog that was so challenging. I didn't know how to handle him so, I just tried to keep him at safe distances from other people and dogs.

Then it happened. I lost control, and Frank attacked another dog. It wasn't bad. He bit the dog once and then stood back with that goofy look on his face—and I knew he was laughing. I went to the vet with the other dog's owner. I tried to say how sorry I was, and as soon as I knew the dog was okay, I paid the bill and went home. Two days later, we were evicted.

A couple of years after that, we're living at another apartment complex. While I was out walking Frank, I saw Anthony walking down the street with the most beautiful little eight week old puppy in his arms. He said that somebody gave him the puppy and asked me if we could keep him. My head immediately said no but my heart took over—and I said yes. Who wouldn't want a puppy? Then, I suddenly remembered who was on the other end of the leash I was holding... Frank.

Knowing what a handful Frank is, I told Anthony the puppy was his responsibility because I could barely handle Frank. He promised he would take care of him and named the little puppy, "Cognac."

It was obvious the puppy was a Boxer, but Anthony said he was only part Boxer.

"What's the other part?" I asked my son. I couldn't believe what I heard when he replied, "Pit Bull." All I can remember after that was my eyes crossing and saying, "Oh Good Lord" and then, everything went blank.

I know that dogs are as individual as people are, but if this little pit bull mix puppy that my son brought home is anything like my pit bull mix puppy that I brought home, it could possibly mean double trouble. I could feel my eyes crossing again.

Chapter Two

COGNAC, A.K.A. PRETTY BOY BABE

I heard that adult dogs won't bite or hurt little puppies because they know they are babies. Only I forgot one very important word..."Generally." What I actually heard was, "Generally, adult dogs won't bite or hurt puppies." That is unless you're Frank.

As much as I hate to admit this, Frank bit little Cognac. And then, stood back like he always did, with that funny look on his face like he was laughing. As I'm trying to comfort the little baby boy, I'm thinking, "What in the world is wrong with you Frank?" Thankfully, it was hardly a bite at all. I think the baby boy was more startled than anything.

In time, Frank accepted Cognac (whom I now call Babe) without any more biting—but, only on his terms. He'd growl at Babe: if he got too close to me; if Babe had a toy; if Babe was eating. It seemed that Frank had to be the boss. He had to call the shots.

If Babe barked at something before Frank barked, Frank would get mad. The two of them then would race outside to the gate, but if Babe got there first, Frank would snap at him. It was bad enough that Babe even barked first, but then, if he got to the gate first too, it must have made Frank look bad. I remember so many times when Frank would take the food bowl right out from under Babe's nose. He would take toys away from him too. Frank would then lay down, put the toy right in front of him, and growl at poor Babe. It was as if Frank were saying, "I double dog dare you."

Babe was such an easy going dog that he let Frank call the shots. One day I was watching the two dogs, just observing their behavior. Babe was having a good time, all by his self, playing with a toy when Frank goes over and takes it from Babe. He then dares Babe to take it back.

Suddenly, Babe barked. Frank took off running to the gate, and Babe got his toy back.

"Atta boy, Babe".

My teenage son was no different than any other, and the promise to take care of Babe the day he brought him home was long forgotten. Now I'm caring for both Frank and Babe. Looking back, I don't know where I got my strength. Both of the dogs were very strong and muscular, Frank weighed in at 65 to 70 lbs. while Babe weighed in at a solid 80 lbs. Both were in very good shape. I'd take them out for walks at the same time, but I'm sure it looked like they were walking me. I liked to take them to the school at night where it was fenced in and safe to let them run. I'd walk around the perimeter. We'd go around ten or eleven pm, because it was less likely for other people or dogs to be there...for Frank to bite. I didn't have to fear for my own safety because I had Frank—and now Babe.

Babe grew up to be an absolutely stunning dog. He looked mostly Boxer, a beautiful fawn with four white socks. People used to tell me all the time how beautiful he was, and some even asked if I wanted to sell him. A very big "no" was my answer every time. He was the exact opposite of Frank. He loved everything and everybody.

He was very laid back and easygoing. He had a comforting way about him and was very in tuned with my feelings and emotions. If I was upset, crying, in a bad mood, Babe would always climb up on my lap and just lay there. Sometimes he'd look up at me and lick a tear or two. Babe was one of the best dogs ever. He was a big love bug.

These two dogs became everything to me. They were my whole world, my whole reason for living. I have suffered with depression my whole life and also became drug addicted and then suicidal. But, no matter how bad things got for me—or how much I wanted to just end my life—Frank and Babe kept me going. I couldn't stand the thought of what would happen to them if I stopped living. I know that Babe would be okay, but on the other hand, there was Frank. He'd surely end up going postal and would probably have to die for his behavior. I couldn't let that happen and so...my life continues.

Living an addicted life equals falling on hard times a lot, an awful lot. And, even though I have a family that is always helping me in one way or another—and desperately wanting me to get help for my addiction—I chose to stay addicted, and while doing so, I fall on hard times again and had to move out of the house where I was living.

I didn't know where I could go now with two large dogs and had been hearing that pit bulls are banned from most rental places. This infuriated me. I couldn't understand. I had met several pit bulls, and every one of them were very friendly.

Nevertheless, I truly didn't know where to go. My family and very few friends said I could come stay with them but, I couldn't bring my dogs. I couldn't leave them either so, we moved into my boyfriend's car. He was away and left his car with me. It might have been selfish of me to put my dogs through this—and this might be selfish thinking—but at that time, I thought they didn't care where we lived as long as we were together. And, thankfully we were together because it was scary, and if I didn't have my dogs, it would've been a hundred times scarier.

My homelessness lasted only a couple of days when a friend took in me and my dogs. But, because Frank liked to bite, both he and Babe had to stay outside in the backyard. I hated it, but, I was in no position to argue it. Thankfully it was a time of year that the weather was nice. Summers in Las Vegas can well exceed one hundred degrees.

I know Frank and Babe didn't understand because they were always allowed in the house and slept with me in my bed. To try to make up for this, I'd hang out with them in the backyard as much as I could, go on more than usual walks every day or I'd take them with me when I could. I don't know if it made them feel better, but it made me feel better…a little better.

I had to sleep in the living room on the floor. I'd have dreams that my dogs and I were all cuddled up together, nice and cozy, just like we always were. Then, I'd wake up and actually find my dogs all cuddled up with me on the living room floor. I wasn't dreaming at all. I don't know how they did it, but somehow they got inside the house to sleep with me.

I can tell my friend wasn't too happy, but I could also tell Frank was turning on his charm (which was a very rare sight) and before long, my friend let them in the house. But, only while I was there.

A short time later, myself and all three of my boys, Anthony, Frank and Babe, were able to move into our own apartment again. I thought everything would be okay now. Only it wasn't okay. I was slipping into my drug addiction even harder. All three of my boys were okay, I thought. But I wasn't. My family said that I looked like the "Living Dead."

Chapter Three

SONYA TO THE RESCUE

One day my sister, Sonya, called me and told me that she found out where I can get help for my addiction—and it wouldn't cost anything. I'm listening to her, but in my mind I'm saying, "Please don't do this! Just accept the fact that I am a drug addict and get off my back" I can hear my sister begging and pleading for me to let her come and pick me up. Without wanting too or even knowing, I said, "You better hurry" and she did.

Now this turned out to be the hardest thing I had ever done in my life because I had to walk away from everything and everybody—including my boys.

In A.A. there are 12 steps to recovery. The first step being the hardest, (*so they say*) "Admitting you are powerless and that your life has become unmanageable". Okay, that was easy enough, I have no problem admitting that. But for me, the hardest step was when I had to take a step out of my three boy's lives, even though it was only temporary.

The plan was that Anthony would take care of Frank and Babe (he was actually the only other person that could handle Frank), and

I was checking into rehab. Turns out though, I ended up checking into Sonya's house because they didn't have a bed available for me at the rehab center. If I would've gone back to where I was staying with my boys, I would've stayed in my addiction.

Sonya and her husband, Ray, and their daughter, Randi, welcomed me into their home and my recovery from drug addiction began. I am excited about a new beginning, but I was also weak, scared, and not really sure if I want to do this or even if I can. But, I kept hearing Sonya begging and pleading with me on the phone that day she picked me up so, I keep telling myself I have to do this.

I missed my boys every second of every day; it was almost more than I can stand. I had to learn to trust God and have Faith. I was told that God knows what He is doing and everything happens for a reason. Sonya kept telling me that I will be blessed for surrendering everything to the Lord and trusting Him.

Did she say, "Surrender?" Is that what I did. I surrendered my three boys? Will God give them back to me?

It turns out that there was no better place for me, and soon I'm able to see how God was working in my life. Starting with, making it possible for me to live with my loving Christian family to help me recover and help my spirit to be fed. The best part to me was that they just happened to have my favorite animals...horses and dogs... to help with my emotional despair. Life cannot possibly get better than this. And then...It does.

My lifelong dream was to one day have my own horse. They are truly the most beautiful and magnificent animals on earth. When I was a little girl, I used to pretend I was a beautiful show horse.

When I was about ten years old, I had a friend named, Rene, and his folks owned a boarding stable for horses. Rene had three ponies: Capricorn, Millie and Teddy Bear. I took a liking to Teddy Bear and spent most of the time with him. He seemed to like me

To The Rescue

too. We used to take the other two ponies to the arena and ride, but Rene hardly ever took Teddy Bear. He said because Teddy Bear was stubborn, nobody could ride him except for Rene—and Rene didn't like to ride him. I felt so sorry for Teddy Bear. So, instead of going with Rene to take the other two ponies out, I'd stay with Teddy Bear. Finally, Rene asked me if I would like to take Teddy Bear out...boy would I ever. I put his bridle on, and we walked to the arena.

Rene gave me a boost on to Teddy Bear and said, "You better be careful."

I rode Teddy Bear further into the arena, down one side, trotted down the other side, and back towards Rene who now stood in disbelief that I was still on Teddy Bear's back.

Sometimes, some of the other kids would ask if they could ride him—and sometimes Rene would let them; but Teddy Bear would get half way down the arena and then he'd stop and roll over every time. He never did that to me. Rene told me that I can have Teddy Bear, but at the same time, he still belonged to Rene. Good enough for me! I finally have my own pony. I'd go to the stables every day and spend every minute that I could with Teddy Bear. I was the luckiest girl in the world.

The fantasy of having my own pony came to an end a short time later because my family moved to another state. I was beyond devastation because Teddy Bear had to stay with Rene.

But years later, while living with Sonya, she told me a friend of hers was giving her a horse, and I know this is God at work again.

He is an Aramis Arabian and his name is "Adeva." Aramis Arabian's are bred by a famous singer that lived and performed in Las Vegas who had a passion for Arabian horses. He actually gave Adeva to my sister's friend which is why she in turn, was giving him away and not selling him.

I spent as much time with Adeva as I could, grooming and

riding him, mucking the stalls, watering and feeding him, or just simply marveling in his beauty. When I was having a bad day—and I had many of them—I'd take Adeva out riding. When I got back, my bad day had turned into a good day. Adeva was good therapy for me.

As much as I loved Adeva and had so much fun with him, he didn't wag his tail or lick my face nor could he sleep in my bed with me. I missed my boys so much it hurt.

A few weeks after moving into to Sonya's house, she told me that she and her husband, Ray, had been talking about bringing my boys over to live with us too, but they would have to stay outside because Sonya had cats and my boys weren't cat friendly. She said that Ray could build them a nice dog run in the backyard, and Ray was even going to build them a nice dog house.

My family truly went above and beyond for me and my boys. I am grateful but also found it hard to believe that all of this was for us. I wasn't used to people who were so loving and kind hearted. People who wouldn't hesitate to make sacrifices for me. Then, it hit me like a ton of bricks: I am being blessed, just like Sonya said.

Ray built a really nice dog run for my boys with plenty of room for them and kept them safely contained. He also built them a dog house to die for. It was fully carpeted from wall to wall and floor to ceiling. He built it big enough for three: Frank, Babe and me. I didn't have to move into the doghouse, but I did stay some nights with my boys in their doghouse from time to time. To me, there was no better feeling in the world than snuggling up with a dog to sleep, content and secure. There are lots of dogs out there that I saw and thought it would be fun to sleep with.

Frank seemed to be mellowing out but sometimes would have a set back and become, "The dude with the 'tude" again. During these setbacks he'd take it out on Babe. A lot of times and always on cold nights, Frank would go into the doghouse and lay right in front of the door so Babe couldn't get in. Babe would stand outside the doghouse and bark at Frank, and Frank would just look at Babe and growl as if he were saying, "C'mon tough boy, I dare you". There were many nights that Ray didn't get any sleep from Babe's barking so we decided to put a divider in the doghouse and added another door.

The blessings keep coming, one right after the other.

Chapter Four

SERENITY BREEZE

My family is super supportive, understanding, and compassionate. They provided everything I needed. They gave me guidance and direction—and everything they ever told me came to be true. I'm clean and sober. Life is good: I have a job at an animal hospital. I have a horse that I get to pretend is mine. My dogs are with me again. What more could I want...a puppy, a pit bull puppy.

I had heard about people abusing and fighting pit bulls, I know if I could have just one, that would be one pit bull who would be safe from the hands of twisted and evil people. The more horror stories I hear, the more I am driven to do what I can to protect and save them.

October 15, 1998, is the day my sweet sister, Sonya, rescued me. October 15th 1999 is right around the corner. My first year of sobriety. Sonya asked me what I wanted for my sober anniversary, and I told her I wanted a pit bull puppy. I actually saw her eyes go cross this time. Sonya and her family included a Great Dane, a Rottweiler mix, seven cats, two horses—and now, myself and my two dogs.

I explained that I thought long and hard about this. I already knew that I could take the puppy to work with me because I often took Frank and Babe, so the puppy would never be alone to destroy things. The puppy would be growing up around cats and other animals so it would be cat and other animal friendly. The puppy could come in the house and sleep with me. I had it all worked out.

I remember one day I was lying in bed with Sonya and some of her animals. I don't know what we were talking, but I noticed a bunch of tiny little scratches on both of her arms.

"What happened to your arms?"

She didn't answer right away, but she got this funny look on her face just like Frank got after he bit somebody. And, with a giggle, she said she got scratched by a rose bush and then started laughing. Then, I started laughing.

"That's a really stupid answer Sonya, cause there aren't any rose bushes anywhere around". Even if there were, you wouldn't see Sonya out there doing the pruning. We were laughing so hard, it hurt. "Sonya, did those scratches on your arms come from a puppy?"

We start laughing again.

On October 15, 1999, for my one year sober anniversary, Sonya handed me a beautiful little female pit bull puppy. She was blond with the blackest mask and mascara on her eyes; she was just beautiful. She was another Blessing from Jesus.

In recovery, I learned the Serenity Prayer and it is my very favorite Prayer still today:

> *"God grant me the **serenity** to accept the things I cannot change; courage to change the things I can; and wisdom to know the difference."*

And, she is named..."Serenity Breeze."

One thing, which I hadn't worked out though, was house training. I didn't know how to crate train at that time, and in the middle of the night, Breeze peed on the carpet a few times. Sonya got upset because the carpet in her house was a very pretty off white, so Sonya booted her to the garage at night—and I went with her. I moved my bed to the garage where Breezy and I slept every night. Even the field mice and Randi's dog, Boogie, joined us. I had put my mattress on the floor of the garage and sometimes, I'd feel the mice scurry across my head late at night, but I didn't care.

Sometimes, Breeze and I would invite Frank and Babe to stay the night. Frank accepted Breeze but didn't really want anything to do with her. He stayed close to me, and Breezy stayed close to Babe. He simply adored her. As time went by, the three of them ended up being pretty good friends.

When Breeze was full grown, she was much smaller than Babe—but I think she had just as much strength. On a cold rainy day, one that you can be comfortable and cozy in sweatshirts and sweatpants, I threw on my sneakers and leashed up Babe and Breeze for their turn to go for a walk to the park. The rain had reduced down to a steady drizzle, but the grass was still very wet. As soon as the dogs and I stepped on the grass, it must have tickled their paws, because they both bolted into a full speed run that I was not expecting. The leashes got wrapped around both of my hands. When they took off, my sneakers slipped on the wet grass. Babe and Breeze dragged me clear to the other side of the park. When they finally stopped my sweatpants (with the elastic waistband) were wrapped around my ankles. I happened to be wearing a thong underwear. To say the least, I was horribly humiliated. Although I didn't see anybody else there, I almost hoped somebody was there and videotaped my body surfing through the park because I am pretty sure it would've won a funniest video award. That was the last time that I ever walked two dogs at the same time.

As Breeze gets older, I start noticing changes in her behavior, like she was testing the waters. She had endless amounts of energy even though we went on walks and sometimes go for a run. I later learned that these changes were red flags. I must admit that my Serenity Breeze was anything but serene.

Chapter Five

DOGS AREN'T THE ONLY ONES

Whenever I saw a stray, pit bull or otherwise, I felt it was my duty to try to help the stray. Chances are the stray will avoid being caught. They're scared, and they don't know I'm there to help—but I still try. If that meant that I would be late for work, so be it.

If I wasn't able to catch them or they would run towards traffic, I'd have to stop and give them to God. I'd close my eyes and hold out my arms as if I were holding the animal, and I'd ask God to take over because I didn't know what else I could do.

Many times, I'd stop and open the back door, and they'd jump right in as if they had been waiting for me to pick them up. I just can't pass by an animal and not do anything. If they were lying dead in the street, I still stop and got them off the street. I don't want it to get run over again and again. If it were my animal, I'd like to think that somebody out there would do the same.

I have a good eye for stray animals, almost like a radar that sends signals to help me find them. One day when I was on my way home from work, I didn't take the normal route that I usually take because something was compelling me to go the other way, so I did. Sure enough, right up ahead of me, I saw three strays. As I got closer to them, I realized it was two dogs trotting down the road with a goat following behind going, "Baaaaaah." I was stumped, to say the least. I can't say that I had ever seen a stray goat before and wasn't quite sure about what to do.

I pulled over and opened the back door. I knelt down and called them to me. They were friendly enough and came right over. I was able to get one dog in the car, but while trying to get the other dog in, the first one jumped out the window. I told myself I would have to come back for him. I managed to get the other dog in my car and decide that I have to get the goat in too cause I couldn't leave him out there. I can't even remember how I did it, but I got the goat in too. I shut the doors and rolled up the windows enough so neither could jump out. I then went back to try to get the first dog who was now standing at a distance watching this comedy unfold. He looked a little confused—heck, I was a little confused myself—now that I had a goat in my car. I could tell that he wanted nothing to do with getting in the car, but I couldn't just leave him out there either. Thankfully, we were out on a back road where there was hardly any traffic. I thought that maybe if I drove slowly, the other dog would want to follow, knowing his friends were in the car...and he did.

So, here I am slowly driving down the road with a dog and a goat in my car, their heads hanging out the window with another dog following. This had to be a funny sight. When I got to my street, I called Sonya and said, "You have to come out front and bring a camera." She watched as I came down the street and saw the dog in one window and a goat in the other with another dog following. The changes in her facial expressions were priceless. We were laughing so hard the tears were running down our face, and every time we looked at my car, we laughed even harder. The three strays were safe.

I remembered when I was out riding Adeva, I saw a goat in an enclosure at somebody's house not far from Sonya's. Surely, they would know other goat people, so I took a chance and drove with my little trio to the house and asked if they knew where the goat and dogs lived. I explained that I found the three trotting down the road, as we walked to my car. Then the guy burst into laughter when he saw the goat in my car, and as if on cue, the goat goes, "Baaaaaah" again. I burst into laughter too. Ironically, that's where they lived. Two dogs and their goat, I was told they were best friends. They made it back home, safe and sound. Only now, I couldn't get the goat out of my car.

I believe that God is what had compelled me to go the other route that day, to rescue those precious animals.

Years before moving into Sonya's house, I was driving on the freeway. It had been raining all day. "My special animal detector" picked up a signal, and I saw a cat laying just beyond the far left lane. I didn't know if the cat was dead or alive. If I would have tried to stop, I'm sure I would have caused an accident with the roads being so wet.

I took the next exit off of the freeway, circled around, and got back on making sure I had enough time to get all the way over to the left so I could stop. Although, this was a dangerous move, I had to get that cat. As safely as I could, I got out of my car and could see the cat was alive. His eyes were the size of quarters, and he was scared stiff. I gently scooped him up and held him tight while we got back into my car. He was cold and wet but otherwise fine. I couldn't find his owner so I kept him and named him "Freeway." He was one of the coolest cats I have ever known.

Another time, I was walking and almost tripped over a pigeon that was obviously in some kind of distress. It appeared that he couldn't fly, but he couldn't walk either. He kept toppling over. I know most people hate pigeons. But not me, not that I like them either. Pigeons are animals too, and I have an obligation to save them.

Sonya used to joke with me and say she had to put me in a cage to keep me safe until I could spread my wings and fly. Sometimes, she let me out of the cage (hypothetically speaking), but if for some reason I didn't do too well on the outside, she would jokingly say, "You gotta get back in the cage."

I'm not going to just leave the pigeon there so I took him home. I borrowed a cage from my neighbor. She also gave me some bird seed that I put next to some water in the cage and then put the pigeon inside. At least for now, he was safe.

The next day, still not knowing what to do, I checked on him. It seemed that he had regained some strength and was now on his feet. Maybe he just needed some rest and he's okay now. I didn't know. I don't know anything about birds. I opened up the cage so he could get out, if he wanted, and then waited to see what he was going to do. After several minutes, he took a few steps outside and then stopped. I waited...then I said, "You gotta do better than that Mr. Pigeon—or you're gonna go back in the cage." With that being said, he spread his wings to fly and fly he did.

Once I saw a young teenage girl walking down the street kicking a dead pigeon with every step she took. I was so mad I could feel my blood boiling. I pulled over and told her to stop or I would have her arrested. I don't think I could've had her arrested, but she didn't know that. Besides, I just happened to be wearing my T-shirt that said, "L.V.M.P.D. K9 Unit (Las Vegas Metropolitan Police Department)" that I got when I went to the K9 police trials. But, she didn't know that either.

To The Rescue

I walked over to one of my friend's house one morning. When we were talking and having coffee, I suddenly felt compelled to go home. I tried to ignore it, but I couldn't. While I was walking home, I could hear a faint sound of an animal in distress. I looked around trying to follow the sound which led me right to a dog that had jumped the fence in his backyard and was hanging on the other side. He had been tied up in his backyard. I felt myself start to panic not knowing what to do. Here was a dog literally hanging before my eyes. Something within me took over and somehow I managed to get the dog down. I think it was just in the nick of time because the dog was giving up the struggle to free himself. The dog fell to the ground gasping for air. After a few minutes, the dog struggled to get on his feet and then walked to the front door of his house. I thought I should knock on the door to let them know what had happened—only the dog wouldn't let me. He'd growl at me every time I took a step closer, and after the last step I took, he tried to charge at me giving me fair warning. I was in shock, but there was nothing more that I could do at that point so I just went home.

Later that same night, I went back to the house. I didn't see the dog so I felt it was safe to knock on the door and let the people know what had happened. I tried to help them with another plan to prevent this from happening again. I told them if they got him neutered, he might stop jumping the fence. I had learned that the majority of dogs that get hit by cars are intact males because they can sense a female dog in heat from miles away. I told them, if they had to resort to tethering him in the backyard, the tether should not be long enough to reach the fence. Years later, tethering became illegal and I am relieved that it is.

Once again, I believe it was God that was compelling me to walk home so I would see another animal in need of help.

There are a lot of times when I simply do not know what to do, whether it was during a rescue or some kind of medical attention that my animals—or family or friends' animals—were needing. Family and friends called me many times asking for help. Although I had worked for a few different veterinarians and took a course on animal care, I never felt that I had the knowledge that was needed. But, often when I was in a panicked state of mind, I could literally feel something take over, a force, and somehow, I'd know what I needed to do.

Sometimes, people would even ask me, "How did you know to do that?"

I can remember saying, "I really don't know" But, I now believe it was God that took over and guided me through. I also believe that rescuing God's precious animals is my purpose in life, my calling. This is what God wants me to do.

Many times though, I didn't necessarily do it the way that God would have wanted me to do it. I might have had to break the law to do it, but I got the job done.

Chapter Six

JESUS SENT JOHN MY WAY

Two years passed from when I first moved into Sonya's. I have been clean and sober for two years. The first time I've ever been clean in my drug addicted career. This was the biggest accomplishment I had ever made. I still remember the first time I walked into an A.A. meeting—and now two years later, I'm chairing the meetings. A.A. was good for me, and the meetings helped me a lot. A.A. is also where I met John, the love of my life.

John worked in construction and could do many things, from building structures to auto mechanics and everything in between. I often thought that I would want to marry a man with many talents. A man like my dad, Don, who wore many different hats. A man like John.

He first came over to meet my family and my dogs. The very next day he came back to do a few improvements on Frank and Babe's run. Summer was coming, and we wanted to make more shade for my boys. Ray and I were in the backyard with John discussing what we wanted and what John had in mind. Before Ray or I could say anything, John opened the gate and entered Frank's run. Mine and

Ray's jaws dropped. We looked at each other in shock, but Frank didn't bite John. Maybe, Frank just didn't bite John yet. This really was out of Frank's character. Ray and I didn't know if we should speak up or not...that might trigger Frank and then he would surely bite. So, we just watched in disbelief. I had not told John yet about Frank liking to bite. He had no clue of the possibilities when he walked through that gate.

We watched as John was going about his business, telling us what he planned for the run and completely ignoring Frank. And the only thing that Frank was doing was sniffing him out. A short time later, John walks out of the run and closes the gate. Ray and I were so relieved that John made it back out alive (so to speak). Frank didn't bite, he didn't try to bite, and I honestly believe, he never even thought about biting.

I have said for many years, "If my dog likes you, then I like you" And, from that day forward, I knew I wanted to spend the rest of my life with my "Man of many talents" John.

Several months later, we married, and Frank still hasn't bit John. The two of them got real close to each other. They are best buds. John even affectionately calls him, "Junior."

We bought our own house and are a family now. A dream come true. And I know that all of this was God's work. Sonya wasn't kidding when she said that I will be Blessed. John is one of my biggest Blessing ever.

Chapter Seven

HELEN READY

After moving out of Sonya's house, most of the dogs that I came upon were strays that got lost. Because they either had on a collar with tags and/or a microchip, I was able to reunite them with their owners. I always got tears in my eyes when their owners picked them up because they were so happy and grateful—and sometimes they would even offer me a reward. Although, the offer was appreciated, I could never accept because I didn't think it was necessary. Some were adamant about it so I would have to suggest that they make a donation to a rescue organization of their choice. Some did, some didn't.

Early one morning, John was leaving for work and found a stray pit bull in our driveway. He came in the house and told me. The two of us went back outside to see what we could do. She had started to wander over to the neighbor's yard, and when she saw us, she cowered.

I always tend to put myself in the animal's shoes, or shall I say paws. I still remember when I was a little girl and my family went to an amusement park—and I got lost. I wasn't hysterical, I wasn't even

crying, but I remember cowering if anybody came towards me. I remember being ashamed, like I did something wrong. It wasn't until my family found me and started scolding me that I started crying, still not knowing what I did wrong. When the stray dog cowered, it broke my heart. Careful not to make any sudden moves, I knelt down and tried to encourage her to me. Reluctantly, she came, and I gave her lots of praise. I told her it was okay, and she was safe now. I asked John to go inside and put our dogs behind closed doors just to be on the safe side. I led her into the house. She had no collar or tags so she got to stay the night. She and I slept in the spare room. The next morning I took her to be scanned, but she didn't have a chip either. I did the usual things when you find a stray; only now that personal computers are in almost every household, there are a lot more resources available. However, I didn't get one phone call, which always surprised me. John and I decided she would stay with us until we could find her a new home.

She had a real pretty red coat so it seemed only appropriate to call her, "Helen Ready." Surprisingly, Frank seemed to have taken a liking to Helen Ready so I teamed the two of them and separated them from Babe and Breeze who were always together. They were in love. I would rotate teams throughout the day so they would all have free time and time outside, similar to crating and rotating without the crate. All the dogs were spayed and neutered so there were no worries there.

The main reason why I decided to separate them, was I already knew how hard it can be with three dogs under my feet which seemed to be at all times. I didn't want to know what it would be like with four dogs. And also, because if a fight broke out, I would have a four dog fight on my hands which I couldn't fathom. Because my three dogs were an established pack already, chances are they would gang up on Helen Ready and I told her she would be safe now. I figured it would be easier to stop a two dog fight opposed to four.

I had learned that Frank still had some bite left in him because he recently bit my father-in-law who is a retired mailman who said he had never been bitten in his whole career as a mailman. Surely, Frank wasn't on his route.

Helen Ready was a little timid and shy but, sweet and non-threatening to Frank, although, I still kept a close eye on him. I don't think he would ever admit it, but I saw a softer and gentler side of him since she first came into our house. I think he might have had a crush on her.

Her stay with us was brief, when she finally got a home of her very own with a young couple that adored her.

Chapter Eight

TROOPER

Every time I get word of an animal in need, without thinking it through, I react...jump right into action...there is no time to waste. Once I get the animal safe, I ask myself the same question almost every time, "What are you going to do now, Miss, here I am to save the day?" Sometimes, I'd just be driving around going nowhere, trying to figure it out. At least the animal was safe.

Sonya called and was telling me that she has a friend who knows of a pit bull puppy that is being abused and neglected—and wanted to know if I could help. Any time one would use the words, "Pit Bull and Abused" in the same sentence, I am always willing to help. By the time Sonya picked me up, I had already changed into my rescue cape and tights with a capital "R" on my chest.

There was no time to waste. She was telling me that she contacted a small independent rescue. They said that they would take the puppy, but we had to transport him to Utah. Sonya already knew about the puppy a day or two before she told me so she had time to make arrangements for the pup. If it had been just me, I'd have the puppy in my car just driving around, probably in circles.

When we got to where the puppy was, I looked around to assess the situation. It appeared that nobody was at home. I have my slip lead in one hand and bolt cutters in the other just in case there's a padlock on the gate. If rescuing this puppy looks urgent, I'll have to cut the lock. Okay, honestly, all I had was a slip lead. A pretty little brindle pup comes to the gate, he looks a little underweight, but otherwise, he looks good and seems happy. There's no lock on the gate so I opened it and slip the lead over his head and walked over to the car with him—and we left.

Piece of cake. I said to Sonya it's good nobody was home because they might have seen us and then be able to identify us. I was glad there wasn't a lock on the gate either because I, in fact, did not have any bolt cutters.

Sonya then looks at me and says, "Why would they do that? They knew we were coming." She forgot to tell me that she had talked to the owners of the puppy, and they agreed to let us come and get him. Sonya and I laughed almost the entire drive to Utah with the puppy we now call, "Trooper." It doesn't matter what Sonya and I are doing, when we're together we always have fun. We could be bored stiff and laughing our heads off.

It was about a three to four hour drive before we came to the small one woman sanctuary. She had five or six individual, chain-linked dog runs. In each run there was a doghouse, and because it was summertime, a small kiddie pool as well. She built her little sanctuary herself, even poured her own concrete. The place was clean, and the animals were happy and healthy. She had a heart like mine, and it was all for the animals.

She inspired me and got me to thinking about all the animals I can save if I just had a nice piece of land. John could build a really nice sanctuary too.

During the drive back, Sonya and I were making up silly names for my imaginary sanctuary like, "Pig Bull Pen" or "Bowman's Barn." We laughed all the way back home

Chapter Nine

MORE THAN ONE

It's funny because my memory is bad. There are times when I can't even remember what I did, said, or heard five minutes ago. But what's funny is that I remember every dog that I've rescued and the reason why. When I was training dogs, I remembered the dog's names but never the client's.

For reasons I cannot remember, I am no longer working at the animal hospital, but I just got a new job as an animal caretaker on a small ranch. It was hard work but still a dream job for me. I like to work hard. I like being outdoors and love working with animals. I fed, groomed, and exercised seven horses, ten dogs, a goat, a pig, and four exotic birds as well as mucked stalls and kept the barn and grounds up to par. I loved this job.

Every day when I'd get to work, as I'm entering the large steel gates, ten dogs would come running down the long driveway to greet me. I can't help but think to myself it would be so cool to have ten dogs (I end up eating those words as time goes by). There are a few big dogs—and a few small—but there's one dog in particular that stands out to me. He is a large, muscular, brindle pit bull, and he exudes confidence and leadership. I felt a little intimidated the first time they came down the driveway to greet me. I remembered when John walked into Frank's run that day, totally ignoring him and he got back out safely, so I completely ignored him and all the dogs for that matter. I was careful not to make any sudden moves. I avoided any eye contact and used caution with every step. I did not want to get on this big boy's bad side.

Then all of a sudden, he bows to the other dogs with his whole butt waggin' in the air, and then he quickly turns to take off running with the other nine dogs chasing him. He was ducking and dodging and twisting and turning. He had moves like a football player. I knew the game he was playing: "Catch me if you can," but none of the dogs could.

I called him, "Boss." I was no longer intimidated. In fact, Boss and I grew very fond of each other. He'd follow me around the barn while I was working and every time I got on the golf cart to go clean up the pastures, Boss sat right next to me. I felt proud to be by his side. I would even take him with me if I had to run to the feed store.

On a long, hot day, Boss and I were on the cart as I was finishing my work. I put my arm around him and said, "Ya know Boss, sometimes they work us like dogs around here." Boss turned and looked at me, and I'm sure he said, "No bull puckey." He was right on cue.

Sometimes on the weekends, John would come to work on the ranch with me. Those were my light duty days because he always did the hardest work for me. Once in a while I'd look to see where he was and what he was doing. I'd often see him on the golf cart heading towards the pastures with Boss sitting right next to him.

Bill, the goat, really took a liking to me too. He wasn't any different from any other goat, but he was always getting into trouble for doing what goats do…chew.

To The Rescue

One of the gardeners would get so mad at Bill. One time I saw the gardener pick up a whip and snap Bill on his rump. I got so mad I picked up a whip and snapped that gardener right back and told him, "How do you like it?"

Several times after that, I would be busy doing my work and I'd hear Bill's little hooves trotting towards me. He'd trot right up behind me like he was hiding. I'd turn around to see what he was hiding from—and here comes the gardener with whip in hand. All I had to do was pick up my whip, and the gardener went the other way.

He is your friend, your partner, your defender, your dog.
You are his life, his love, his leader.
He will be yours, faithful and true, to the last beat of his heart.
You owe it to him to be worthy of such devotion.
~~Unknown~~

Chapter Ten

THE SO-CALLED NO KILL SHELTER

Working on the ranch was a temporary job that only lasted a few months. I miss working there, and I miss Boss too, but it was time to move on.

I saw an ad in the paper for an intake and impound receptionist at the new local no-kill shelter. This would be perfect for me so I applied. I don't think I would have applied had it been a kill shelter. But, the ad read, clear as day, "No Kill Shelter."

I was hired, and my job was to do all the data entry work for every animal that came to the shelter, whether it be by animal control or dropped off by whomever. I also did data entry for impounding, quarantined, and return to owners, along with animal licensing, vaccination, and rabies certificates.

Every single night after work, I drove home in tears. I could not believe how easy it was for some people to just dump their dogs at the shelter. In the dog's eyes were utter fear and confusion. The owners found it amusing to have to literally drag the dogs in.

I'll always remember one dog named "Pinto" because he was so scared he came in on his nails. I don't think his paw pads even touched the ground. His owner was laughing, and it made me mad. I asked the owner what was so funny, but he didn't speak English, so I took the leash out of his hand and made him leave. Pinto was a pit bull, and my heart was breaking for him. I had my own office at the shelter so I managed to get Pinto in my office and laid out blankets on the floor. I shut the door and laid on the floor with Pinto. He was still shaking and still had fear in his eyes. I tried so hard not to cry while I held this baby in my arms to comfort him, but my emotions were out of control. I could feel his fear. I could feel his pain. I couldn't understand how his owner could not.

I tried to keep him with me for as long as I could. He was even starting to relax a little, but the shelter manager said he had to go to the kennels. I knew all of the fear and confusion would come right back to poor Pinto. I begged her to let him stay a little bit longer. I told her how he came in and how terrified he was. She simply said that most of them come in the same way. She then put a leash on him and walked out of my office with him walking on his nails again. I hated her.

The only thing I could think of to do was to stand with my arms out as if I were holding Pinto, and I gave him to God. I gave a lot of them to God.

I couldn't wait to get to work the next morning so I could check on him and see how he's doing—maybe sneak him into my office for a little while. But when I got there, Pinto was nowhere to be found. I asked around but nobody knew anything.

It didn't take long for me to learn that this shelter was not what they claimed to be. It was a kill shelter, and I didn't want to work there anymore. I was told that there is no such thing as a "No kill shelter." The difference between where I worked and the other shelters was that we didn't have a contract with the city or county that would force us to euthanize animals for lack of space. The only animals that we did euthanize were either deathly ill or critically injured, and it would be the only humane thing to do. But this was not true either.

I overheard the shelter manager talking with another manager about a euthanasia list. When I asked my coworker what they were talking about, she told me they were making a list of animals to kill. I started to say I thought this was a no kill shelter when she cut me off and said, "We all thought…" I didn't have to ask what happened to Pinto any more. I think I knew, and it pains me to even write those words. I didn't even get to tell Pinto goodbye. I thought I would see him again the very next morning. I couldn't get the fear in his eyes out of my mind. If I could've just been able to hold him one more time and tell him I love him and he's a good boy. My eyes welled up, and I felt sick to my stomach. Probably, much like Pinto on his last day.

Who could even make that kind of decision anyway? We had hundreds of animals, most of them were pit bulls and cats, but the amount of them that were sick or injured did not add up to the amount of animals that were going on the list.

Although I didn't want to work there anymore, I decided, somehow, I had to make a difference. I was going to do it in Pinto's honor. In honor of all the animals that had to die at a shelter.

This was the most emotionally overwhelming job I have ever had, and I truly did cry every night on my way home. It was how I released all the tears I fought back throughout the day. A lot of times I'd call Sonya on my way home to tell her about my experiences. I couldn't understand how people could be so cold hearted. I kept thinking, if they would just put themselves in their animal's shoes, like I always do, they could feel their animal's fear, their pain, their confusion. If people could just do that, they would never dump their animals and then find it amusing.

I heard so many horror stories about how people would treat

their pets. A lot of the animals that came to the shelter wore the evidence physically, emotionally, or both. The sad and lonely lives of "backyard dogs."

Why even have a dog if he cannot be a member of your family?

The abuse some dogs had endured because the owners didn't know how to house break them or stop them from digging or barking. Why get mad at the dog for what you don't know?

I'd see animals that were lucky enough to get adopted, leave the shelter with their new owners only to come back two days later and have to go through the trauma all over again. My heart broke for every one of them. I heard the lamest excuses why they brought them back. I felt that the people in adoptions were failing these animals and probably weren't doing a very good screening or counseling of potential adopters, if they even did it at all.

When I think I've heard every story imaginable, I hear more—even more horrific. While working at the shelter, I learned about "bait dogs." I couldn't even comprehend this. Not only did I learn about it but actually seen some bait dogs with my very own eyes. These were visions that even years later haunt me. "Who"… "Why"… "What is wrong with people?"

Another pit bull that would stay in my heart forever, along with Pinto, was a little female who I called "Red." She was a bait dog. She was brought by animal control who had picked her up after receiving a call about alleged dog fighting. She was the first bait dog that I actually seen with my own eyes. This baby was literally chewed up, spit out, and then stomped on. As I looked at this innocent being, cowering in the corner as if she had done something wrong, I could feel my blood boil. I couldn't express the anger I felt and, even worse, I knew she would have to go to sleep.

One could only speculate what all Red had been through. I tried to imagine myself being Red: savage, vicious dogs chewing me up while screaming out… "What did I do?" I had to stop imagining, it was more than I could handle. Much like it was for Red, only for her, it was real. I wondered why somebody didn't ever love her enough to protect her. Did she ever feel human kindness? Who could do this to her and, why, why, why?

I wanted to hold her so bad, but I was afraid I'd hurt her. I looked into her eyes that seemed to be pleading with me to love her. Truth was, I loved her the exact moment I first laid eyes on her, but then, how could she know that?

Knowing what her fate would be, I knew I was destined for her to be loved, to feel love, maybe for the first time in her life. I bent down to see if she would come to me. Still cowering, she managed. "Good Lord, is she thinking I'm going to throw her back to the dogs that chewed her up." "Is that why she's still cowering?" "Oh my gosh!"

As gently as I could, I picked her up and carried her to my office. I threw some blankets on the floor, which I kept in my office ever since for Pinto. I shut the door and gently laid her down. I fluffed up the blankets to make her as comfortable as I could. I then laid down with her. I told her how beautiful she was and she's a good girl. I told her how sorry I was that this happened to her and how much I love her over and over again. This innocent, beautiful, little girl took every bit of strength she had left and inched her way into the crook of my arm. She then licked my face while the tiny tip of her tail wagged slightly. With a painful sigh, she laid back down in my arms. I could no longer hold back my tears. As busted up as Red was, she managed to give me a kiss and wag her little tail. I know she was saying, "Thank you."

When the vet came in, she said what I had already known, Red had to go to sleep. I didn't want her to be moved. She was comfortable and I wanted to stay with her to the very end so I asked the vet if she would do the procedure right there where we were. She started to say, "Connie," but I stopped her and said, "Please… if Red had to go to sleep, I wanted her to go with my love." She said that we could get in trouble. "I can handle trouble, but there's no way I could handle letting Red go alone and without love." The vet was hesitant but then said okay.

While I held Red in my arms, telling her how much I love her, she gently and peacefully went to sleep. Her misery was over.

I would like to think that at some point in Red's life, somebody loved her. This got me into thinking about how many animals didn't know what love felt like.

It was then that I realized how I can make a difference in the shelter where animals live and die. There were so many of them that never knew what love felt like and had to go to sleep at no fault of their own. From that day forward, I made sure they went with my love. Many people asked me, "How can you do that?" "How can you hold the animals when they were being euthanized?" My only answer was, "How can I not."

The shelter where I work was a fairly new facility with state of the art of everything. However, the location of the shelter was not in the best area of the town. One day while at work, I was having a super stressed-out day and had to take a break from everything. I went outside to relax a little and regain my composure. All of a sudden, I heard gunshots that couldn't be very far away from where I was. I looked across a small empty lot toward the sound of the gunshots and I saw a dog running fast with his tail tucked between his legs.. Not being in a good state of mind already, I took off running toward the dog. I've got to save him or he's going to get shot. Running right behind the dog was the shooter firing another shot. I was freaking out, yelling and screaming at the shooter some obscenities I have never heard before. Then, I couldn't see the dog anymore. I was thinking I was going to find him shot to death.

Oh my gosh, this cannot be happening.

An animal control officer had heard that gunshots were fired. He quickly pulled up behind me and somehow got me in his truck. I couldn't go any further. I was begging and pleading with him to help me save the dog and he said, "I have to save you first." I was enraged. The dog's safety should've come first, isn't that why we worked at the shelter? To save and protect the animals. I promised him I would stay in the truck if he would just try to find the dog, but I didn't. I went looking for him too, but we never found him.

I've told my family many times prior to this, if we are ever in a position where an animal and I are both in a life or death situation at the same time, help the animal first and then come back to help me because if they don't, I would be as good as dead anyway.

Word got back to my boss and I was called into the office. She said, "That was a stupid stunt." I said, "Maybe it was." She said, "I'm not happy about this." I said, "Neither am I." That was all either of us said.

The emotional roller coaster that I rode every day was taking a toll on me and I didn't know how much more I could take. The bad days outweighed the good days that were far and few between, but at least there were some.

The managers put together a "fun day" event to promote animal adoptions. They reduced the adoption fees, vaccination fees, and spay/neuter fees. They had educational booths, face painting for the kids, and clowns with balloons. They had a doggie talent and fashion show with some of the dogs that were up for adoption. Some of the employees, including myself, were allowed to pick a dog from adoptions to work with. One might think that would be easy enough, but it wasn't, for me anyway.

Just like there were many times that I wanted to adopt them all, I also wanted them all to be in the show, it seemed only fair. To have to choose just one meant the others' feelings would be hurt. Much like when I was a little girl–everything had feelings, from every living being to my blanket to the wallpaper. I was very careful that no feelings were ever hurt. I even caught myself trying to sneak a dog out while I thought the others weren't looking.

Do I need to "get a grip?" Probably.

In adoptions I found a beautiful golden brindle pit bull and I named her "Honey." She was super sweet and outgoing. She could care less what you were doing to her—a little tug on her ear, a slight pinch on her toes–she didn't care, she just loved the attention. For the next week, Honey got to hang out with me every day. We were going to be in the fashion show so we had to practice walking down the runway.

I have always been a t-shirt and jeans kind of girl and when John and I first met, one of his favorite songs was "Tiny Dancer." Some of its lyrics are "Blue jeans baby... L. A. lady." I chose Tiny Dancer for our theme song. I got Honey a little denim skirt and a white t-shirt to go with my jeans and white t-shirt and we became "The Blue Jean Babies." I had so much fun at work that week and a lot of animals were adopted.

I got pretty attached to Honey. I even wanted to adopt her myself but I still had my three pets at home that kept me busy enough. Although I thought when you have three already, what's one more?

I wondered all weekend long if Honey got adopted. She was so cute as The Blue Jean Baby, I just knew that she did. I looked for her on Monday morning when I went back to work, she wasn't there. I didn't dare ask.

Chapter Eleven

Two Great Danes and a Spot

S onya's favorite breed is Great Dane. She rescued her first Dane from a pet store. She named him "Daney the Great." He was a beautiful blue merle. He was Sonya's heart, her everything, and her world. When he was a puppy, Sonya and her family were going out of town so I babysat for her. I had very strict instructions on putting him down for a nap. She didn't want his routine to be broken. Although he was just three or four months old, he was already the size of an average adult dog. Actually, he was even bigger and was perfectly capable to jump up on the bed himself. He just didn't know it because Sonya would always pick him up and put him down for his nap, regardless that he already weighed 200 pounds. It was in her instructions as well so that's what I did. I would sing a song I wrote for him and he would calm down and fall right to sleep.

Daney grew into a slightly larger than normal Great Dane. If you can imagine that, they are already big, what could even bigger look like? He had a growl that would stop anybody in their tracks and a bark that would knock you off your feet. Sonya would sometimes call him Lurch, from the Adam's Family T.V. show. Sonya taught me about Danes. You wouldn't think this by their size but they are very sensitive. They like to lean on their owners and to back right up onto your lap and sit as if they were a lap-size dog. Sonya would say, "He doesn't know he's big."

Because of their size, the average life span for a Great Dane is seven to ten years and that might even be pushing it. Unfortunately, when Daney was only about seven years old, he was diagnosed with a rare immune disorder. At one point, he even needed a blood transfusion and Randi's dog, Boogie, was the donor.

Sonya did the best that she could do and then had to make that dreaded decision to let him go to sleep. To say that she was devastated would be an understatement. She was beyond devastation and for months to follow, she was not herself at all. She was in terrible pain and I wanted to take that pain away.

I have always said that when one loses a beloved pet, the best thing to do is get another. But try not to replace the one that has passed for there is no replacement. There is a dog out there somewhere that desperately needs to be rescued, and when one would do so, that dog in turn rescues one. This is tried, tested, and true.

Sonya said that in time she would get another Great Dane so when a Great Dane came into the shelter, I knew it was time. There is a seventy two–hour hold on all the lost animals that come to the shelter. This means that the owners have to claim their animals within seventy two hours. If not, the shelter becomes the owner and hopefully, the animal will then go into adoptions.

As soon as the hold was lifted and I knew the Dane was available for adoption, I brought him into my office and called my devastated sister. I told her we have a Great Dane that needs a new home.

She said she wasn't ready, but in the same breath she asked

several questions. "Is it male or female?" She and I are partial to males.

"He's a male."

"What color is he?" "Black." Again, she said she wasn't ready. "But wait… Why is he there?"

"He was lost but never claimed."

"He's been here for four days, and he's lost a lot of weight."

"I'm on my way," she said. I said, "You can name him Connor, after me." She did.

The next day, I had to go and pick up dogs from an animal hospital that were picked up by animal control after shelter hours, but were injured and needed medical attention. One in particular was a white Pit Bull/Boxer that had been hit by a car. His white coat was covered in black road rash as if he had rolled on impact. He had an injury to his back leg that he carried and both of his ears were infected from being "scissor cut" and sutured with string. In spite of it all, it was love at first sight.

I asked the vet what was meant by "scissor cut." The vet told me that it was a common thing that the gangs do. This is even hard for me to write. While a couple of scumbags hold a dog, another scumbag cuts his ear flaps off with household scissors and then sews them with any kind of string. They cut them almost completely off to prevent them from being torn off in a dog fight. It makes no sense at all. Like unprofessionally cutting them off with household scissors is better than being torn off.

How could it get any worse than that? Who in their right mind could do something so barbaric? I tried to imagine being this innocent creation of God, but it is inconceivable to me. What is wrong with these people? Why, why, why? I feel somewhat ashamed to be of the human kind.

I was looking at this poor dog and he was looking back at me. In his eyes, I saw forgiveness. He lived in the moment. He would be a much better person than I am myself. I wished I could find the punks that did this and cut their ears off with household scissors. I wished that there was a universal law—a law that is described as "An eye for an eye."

It became quite clear to me that my heart bleeds the most over the dogs that have endured the most. The ones like Red who were chewed up, spit out, and stomped on—the ones who suffered the most trauma. But why? I kept trying to analyze this over and over. It occurred to me that I wanted to make it up to them. I wanted to right all the wrongs that had been done to them.

I didn't know how I'm going to tell John, but I have to have this dog.

When I got back to the shelter, I gave him a bath. I was careful around his ears so they wouldn't get wet, they were painfully sore and infected. He seemed to really enjoy it. It had to feel good to get all cleaned up. I was surprised to see after all the blackness washed off of him how beautiful he was. He was all white and he had a round brown spot that covered his left eye. I didn't have to put any thought into a name—he was wearing it, "Spot." He was actually stunning.

From the bath, we went into my office where Spot laid comfortably on some blankets while I tried to get caught up on my work. Dr. L. came in to examine Spot and she said, "It doesn't look good." Stunned by what she said, I said, "What are you talking about?" "He can recover from his injuries, he's not as bad as poor Red was." Dr. L. agreed but further explained that the shelter is not going to want to cover the cost for Spot's medical needs. How does this stinking shelter claim to be a no-kill shelter? They've lied about it from the very beginning. Had they told the truth, I would have never applied, but then I wouldn't have been able to help these innocent animals.

The thought never once crossed my mind that Spot would be euthanized. If it did, I wouldn't have taken any chances, I would've taken him straight to my house. I would've covered the cost of his medical needs myself and he would never have seen the inside of a shelter. Sure, there would be consequences and I'd deal with it. I'm good at that.

Dr. L. knew that I was already attached. She said, "I'll do what I can." In the meantime, she agreed to let Spot stay in my office. I posted notices on the shelter doors for anybody who had lost a white Pit Bull/Boxer to see me. Not that I wanted his owners to find him, if they did, I planned on interrogating them and filing animal cruelty charges. Just in case somebody was looking for Spot, they wouldn't find him in lost and found, and legally they still had seventy two hours. I told Dr. L. if nobody claims him, I wanted to adopt him and I would do whatever I have to, to save him.

When I went home that night, I told John all about Spot. John was very empathetic until I asked him if I could bring him home. He got a little irritated and said, "You can't save them all."

I didn't expect this kind of reaction. I was very upset, and I went to bed crying. The next morning, John was in the shower and he yelled out, "Connie, you better go and get that baby before something terrible happens," and I was out the door. This is one reason why John is the love of my life.

Spot had surgery that same day. He had to be neutered and the strings in his ears had to be surgically removed.

When I got off from work, I took my dog Spot and we went home.

Chapter Twelve

THE DAILY JUGGLE

When John got home from work, he couldn't believe his eyes when he saw Spot. John was so cute when he knelt down to pet him and said, "Come here baby. It's okay." Spot loved the attention.

I didn't want to put Spot with the other dogs yet because he just had surgery so I set up my office at home nice and cozy for him. My office sets right off of the living room and has French doors. The middle of the doors is glass so even with them closed, you can still see in and out. When we first bought this house, I didn't like the glass doors because I feared the dogs playing could accidently break them and end up getting cut. But John explained that the glass is tempered so the doors are more durable than they look. Now I like the doors because I think they're perfect. If I have to separate the dogs, the dogs won't feel isolated from us because they could still see us through the glass.

At that time, the only thing in my office was a sofa. Every day when John and I would come home from work, we saw less of the sofa than the day before. I worried what John would say, but he simply blamed it on Spot still being a puppy. Spot was about a year old.

My dogs, or any other dog that comes into my home, are allowed to stay on the furniture and to sleep on our bed. However, there is not enough room on a king-size bed for John, me, and the three medium-to-large-sized dogs. Somehow, John and I would end up teetering on the very edges of the bed. So we decided that Frank got to sleep with us at night because he was the oldest, and he came first. Babe and Breeze had each other so they got the spare bedroom with their own bed. They were in love and inseparable from the very moment Breeze came into our lives.

Babe used to groom Breeze from head to toe for what seemed like hours. She loved every second of it.

I never worried one time about the two of them ever getting into a fight. But, my sweet little Serenity Breeze wouldn't hesitate going after Frank if he did something to Babe that she didn't like. They never got into a fight, but it was clearly a possibility so I had to keep a close eye on them during the day. If I had to leave the house, I put Frank in my room and closed the door. Frank didn't seem to mind being singled out. It appeared that he enjoyed his solitude.

After a couple of weeks of recovery for Spot, I carefully introduced the dogs one at a time. They all knew each other because they saw each other every day through the glass doors. The introductions went well to my relief, but, once again, I teamed the dogs up. On one team was, of course, Babe and Breeze, and the other was Frank and Spot. I kept them separated and rotated them throughout the days. To my surprise, it seemed that Frank liked Spot, but I knew Frank could be a tricky one so I kept a close eye on them. If I had to leave the house, Frank would go into my room, Spot would go into the office, and Babe and Breeze would go wherever they wanted in the rest of the house.

It seemed that Breeze was starting to develop some mild dog aggression toward Frank and Spot—mild, but enough to concern me. After what I had already gone through with Frank, I had to nip this in the bud right away so I enrolled Breeze into obedience training. The trainer's name was Mike who did a phenomenal demonstration with his dogs.

I told him that I was seeing some dog aggression with Breeze—and I had three other dogs. I further explained how I raised her with nothing but love and how she grew up with other dogs, cats, and horses. I just didn't understand where the aggression was coming from. I had heard other pit bull owners say, "It's all in how you raise a pit bull." Mike used to have a pit bull. He told me that how you raise a pit bull, or any other dog for that matter, is only a part of it. How well they are bred plays a very important factor as well. Professional breeders know how to produce sound and stable puppies, whereas backyard breeders are defeating their whole purpose and are only trying to make money. They have no clue what they are doing, nor do they care. Breeze was a product of a backyard breeder.

He then worked with Breeze and within a matter of minutes, I saw results. As sweet and loving as she is, she can also be a hellion. As I watched the trainer handle her with ease, I couldn't stop the tears that had welled up in my eyes. It was a beautiful sight to see. I worried when he walked her around his dogs, but he was in total control. His training wasn't cheap but proved to be a very good investment.

Chapter Thirteen

THE INEVITABLE

Mike suggested that I put a basket muzzle on Breeze to be on the safe side. It broke my heart when she desperately tried to paw it off, but Mike said this was normal behavior for dogs wearing a muzzle for the first time. The basket muzzle fit loose enough so she could pant and even drink water, but snug enough so if she were to bite, it would only be a nip. We trained in a group class at a park. Whenever another dog got close to Breeze, I could feel her low growl vibrate through the leash, but after a quick correction, she'd be okay again.

One day in training, we all had our dogs in a sit/stay. We then walked a few feet away from them. I tried to carefully watch Breeze's body language in these kind of exercises, but she saw an opportunity to attack another dog in our class. I was about to panic, but I remembered she had a muzzle on. I was able to regain control over her pretty quickly, but I knew if she didn't have a muzzle on, it could've been very ugly. It still upset me.

Mike suggested that I put a long line on Breeze during training, which is basically a fifteen feet or longer leash. That way, I will have better control when we practice things like the sit/stay.

I started taking Spot to training too. We trained three to four times a week. I would take Breeze one day and Spot the next. Breeze and Spot also took their CGC (Canine Good Citizen) test the same day and both passed. They were Certified Canine Good Citizens.

I thought taking my dogs to the dog parks was a responsible thing to do as a pit bull owner and a good way to socialize them. I always kept a close eye on my dogs and their body language, careful to avoid any fights, but I noticed that not everybody did the same. It seemed to be a social hour for the dog owners as well. One day, I took Spot to the dog park. Upon entering, two young pit bulls tried to double team him so I immediately took him back out and put him in a sit/stay. Keeping an eye on him, I then went to talk to the young pit bull's owner. I was very nice and simply asked her to not let her dogs double team my dog for fear that a fight would entail. She was very snooty and replied, "They are only nine months old. What could they possibly do?" I told her that it was all the more reason to have control of her dogs. Usually, around that age, dogs are trying to find their independence. In a snooty way, she said she would watch her dogs.

I should've known better. I went back to Spot and together we went back into the park without any trouble. Until we were about midway in, the same two pit bulls double teamed Spot again. Fortunately, I was able to back them off and got Spot out of the park while cursing at the owner of the dogs.

With Spot on a leash, we preceded to just walk on the paths of the park. A few minutes later, the owner of the young pit bulls approached me and said, "Your dog made one of my dogs bleed."

I replied, "I'm sorry, but it's not my problem. I tried to tell you what potentially could happen."

She then asked me what I was going to do about it.

I said, "Nothing."

She threw a few choice words at me that I blocked with, "You shouldn't even have pit bulls, because you obviously are not responsible enough. You're just contributing to their already bad reputation."

She then swung on me. The two of us were in a fist fight in the park. I am not trying to toot my own horn, but after the cops were called and witnesses told them the other woman threw the first punch, I told them I didn't want to press charges. I walked away unscathed. I cannot say the same for her. That was the last time that I took any of my dogs to the dog park.

Although Breeze didn't seem to love training the way Spot did, he was animated, outgoing, focused, and excelled in training. I was having more fun training Spot. Without realizing it at that time, I took Spot to training more often than Breeze. Eventually, I quit taking Breeze altogether. That was a huge mistake.

I remember when I first got Breeze. She went to work with me every day and made the garage our bedroom. She was my baby girl—we were inseparable. A year or so later, Spot entered our world. Little by little, Spot took all of my attention away from her. How I wish I would've seen it sooner.

Ultimately, Breeze got jealous and hated Spot. Every chance she got, she would attack him.

Chapter Fourteen

LOOKING THROUGH HER EYES

I've been trying to write this chapter for over a month now. I realized that while writing this book, I was also re-living everything I've written about. Some happy, some sad—but this one is especially hard for me. I don't want to re-live the events that took place. It's been almost eight years ago, but I am still traumatized by it all.

Frank and Spot, for the most part, got along really good, but Frank is Frank. One day, Spot had enough of Frank's bullying. The two dogs were ready to fight. As Frank was charging toward Spot, I picked up Spot and kind of tossed him behind me at the same time that Frank lunged in to bite Spot. His mouth bit down the back of my arm. I screamed out in agony. It felt like he ripped the flesh right off the bone.

Thankfully John was home and came running out when he heard me screaming. The pain was excruciating. I couldn't breathe or talk. I think I was passing out. John quickly figured out the boys had got into a fight. He was able to get them separated and behind closed doors. He then came back to check on me. The back of my arm was on fire. I was afraid to see what the damage was. After John looked at it, he said I have to go to the hospital. There were three punctures, and one of them was bleeding.

Knowing that hospitals report all dog bites to animal control, which quarantines the animal for ten days, I decided not to go to the hospital. I tried to take care of the wounds myself, but I ended up going to the hospital anyway.

There was no denying that the wounds were from a dog bite, so I told John that we were not going to say it was our dog that bit me. I lied and said I tried to break up two dogs that got into a fight, but I did not know the dogs or who they belonged to and that I never had seen them before. I didn't know if the doctor believed me or not. I didn't even care. I just did not want my dogs quarantined for something I should not have gotten into in the first place.

To prevent this from happening again, I put a mesh muzzle on Frank whenever he and Spot were together. Spot wasn't the kind of dog that would bully other dogs—we all know that Frank is.

Frank, Spot, and I were in the backyard one day while I was doing yard work. Frank had his muzzle on. I went inside the house for something. When I came back outside to the backyard, Breeze slipped through the door and attacked Spot. Frank tried to get in the fight as well. I heard one loud yelp, and then he disappeared. Babe came outside and started to get in the fight, but somehow I managed to get him back inside the house behind closed doors. I went back outside and saw Breeze and Spot tearing each other literally apart. The vicious sounds of the growling and snarling still echo in my mind today. I couldn't get them to stop no matter what I tried. I was screaming at the top of my lungs for somebody to help me, "They're going to kill each other!" I took off running through the house to the front yard where I suddenly just dropped. I was helpless. I didn't know what to do. I knew they were going to kill each other.

My neighbor came out. I told her to call John for me. I could still hear the vicious growling. I covered my ears. I couldn't stand it. My dogs were going to be dead the next time I'd see them.

It seemed like hours had passed by, although it was about twenty minutes later. My neighbor's son looked over the wall into my backyard. He said he couldn't see them. There was no more growling. I couldn't hear anything. I knew they were dead.

"I see them. They're not fighting anymore," my neighbor's son said.

I asked him what they were doing.

He replied, "Nothing, just standing there."

Standing there? That means they're not dead.

John pulled up, and the two of us ran to the backyard. I remembered seeing blood everywhere as I ran through the house. I remembered fearing the worst. We got to where Breeze and Spot were. They were a bloody mess and breathing hard from exhaustion, but they were alive. I grabbed Breeze and put her in my car. John grabbed Spot and put him in his truck. Then we went to find Frank who was lying in a corner of the backyard. He couldn't get up. His leg was broken. He still had his muzzle on. John put him in his truck, and we raced to the animal hospital. On the way, I called the hospital to let them know we were coming in with three fight victims. They met us in front of the hospital and immediately took the dogs in one by one.

That was when I lost it and fell to my knees. I couldn't believe what had just happened. I could still hear the vicious growling and snarling. I covered my ears again.

Finally, Dr. A. came out to talk to us. He said, "It's not good. They're in shock and pretty torn up." I was so scared and sick to my stomach. I was going to throw up. Again, I couldn't breathe. I could still hear the growling.

Dr. A. said we needed to go home and wait for his call. I didn't want to go, but his instructions were firm.

There was blood everywhere—on the floors, walls, doors, windows, furniture, patio, grass—everything was blood red.

I remembered Babe was in one of the rooms. I completely forgot. I didn't even know if he was hurt, but I looked him over and ran my hands all over his body in case there was something I couldn't see. He was fine. I grabbed and held onto him sobbing like never before. Babe laid with me holding onto him for a very long time. Thank God he wasn't hurt. Every now and then, he would lick my tears. There was no other dog that was as comforting as my Baby Boy. I could've stayed right there holding onto him forever. I wanted to stay there. I didn't want to see all the blood again. I didn't want Babe to see it either.

I left the bedroom and found my sweet husband cleaning up the mess.

Thank you Jesus for my husband.

At this point, I've come to the realization how stupid it is to have four dogs. I have always believed in having at least two dogs so they would never have to be alone—more than two is insane. It is impossible to give each what is required to have a healthy and happy dog. It's a lot of work and stress. It is not fair to either the dogs or anybody else.

Chapter Fifteen

DAMAGES

Later that night, Dr. A called. He said the three of them were stable but had to be in intensive care for a few days. Breeze and Spot had to have emergency surgery. They were torn up pretty bad around the face and head. He placed tubes in the wounds so they would drain and prevent infection. He also sutured some of the gashes. Breeze had a skull fracture and had lost a canine tooth. Her other tooth had been knocked loose so he had to extract it. Spot was chewed up pretty bad but not as bad as Breeze.

Frank's injury was a broken leg. The middle part of his front leg had been crushed. I remembered Frank was wearing a muzzle so he never had a chance to defend himself.

How stupid could I be? This is insane. What was I thinking?

I asked Dr. A if his leg could be repaired. He said he wanted to x-ray his hind quarters to make sure that they could support his front leg, which now would be lame. He said we had to consider Frank's age (he was fourteen). When Frank turned twelve, I thought it would be a good idea to try to mentally prepare myself for the day I'd have to let him go. I was not prepared for this. I don't know how to make the decision. Frank has been with me for so long, and now it's coming to an end.

Is this really happening?

Dr. A said I could come see my babies in the morning. I was the first person there. The hospital wasn't even open yet.

John called Sonya and told her what happened. We met at the hospital. They put us in an exam room and brought Breeze in. Breeze looked like a monster. There was a look in her eyes that I didn't recognize—her eyes looked wild. It was very strange, almost eerie.

There were sutures and tubes protruding from her wounds that were all over her face, head, and legs. She was so swollen. I wanted to hold her close to me, but I was afraid to touch her in fear of hurting her even more. I got down on the floor, and she climbed into my lap.

I could see the pain she was in. I would've given anything to take her pain away. I cried and told her how sorry I was. It was all my fault. I should've kept training her—it was working. I should've never let Spot come between us. I should've never had so many dogs. I cried and cried. I promised her I would never have so many dogs at one time again. I didn't see it then how she was hurting for me, but it's all so very clear now. I know how jealousy feels and it doesn't feel good. It hurts—it hurts really badly.

They took Breeze back and brought Spot in. He too looked like a monster. His eyes looked even wilder. The staff said they had him on a special diet, but he wouldn't eat. I asked them to bring me some of his food because I wanted to try to hand-feed him. At first, he refused so I pretended to take a bite of it myself and then offered some to him. Reluctantly, he took a small bite, then turned his nose so I had to take another bite and he ate some more. I had to repeat this until the food was gone. I asked Dr. A. why Breeze's and Spot's eyes looked the way they did. He said it was from the heavy doses of pain medication they were receiving. I was a bit relieved. Dr. A. said he wanted to keep them hospitalized for a few more days. Again, I was relieved. I wasn't ready to bring them home. I was afraid.

How can I afford this?

I didn't know. All I knew was I was scared to bring them home.

The staff took Spot back and brought Frank in. He had a cast on his front leg but was able to walk on his own. They brought in a blanket for him to lay on the floor. Sonya and I laid on the floor with him. Dr. A. explained how Frank's leg was literally crushed. Right at that moment, I noticed that Frank didn't have a muzzle on. It occurred to me that the staff was even petting him. I was sure I told them all that Frank would bite, but he didn't. I looked at him, and there was that goofy look on his face.

Dr. A said that the x-rays on Frank's hips and back legs showed signs of old age. He said they would not be strong enough to support his crushed front leg even if they did extensive surgery. He said that the quality of Frank's life would not be good. Considering his age of fourteen years, Frank had surpassed his life span by two years. Dr. A said, "If Frank were my dog, I would let him go to sleep." I just got hit by a train.

I looked at Frank. He still had that goofy look on his face and was wagging his tail. I looked at Sonya who was already crying with me. I said, "I don't know how to let him go." But I did. I stayed with Frank. I held and told him how much I loved him. I thanked him for loving me and that it was an honor that he did. I kept telling him over and over to the very end.

I was numb. I couldn't feel anything, but again I heard the growling. Then I heard that one yelp, which must have been coming from Frank when they crushed his leg. He still had that stupid muzzle on, which I put on him. It was more than I could take. I ran—I ran to what I knew best: drugs.

I got high. I was still numb even without drugs. It was good. I didn't want to feel. I didn't want to think. I didn't want to go through any of this. I was beating myself up for being so stupid, for having too many dogs—and for throwing my sobriety away. I didn't care about my sobriety though. I just wanted to stay high.

Where did I go wrong? How could I have prevented this? Why did I have to muzzle Frank? Oh my gosh, I'm never going to see Frank again. I wanted to die. I wanted to be with Frank.

Could the negativity about bully breeds be true? Am I out of my league? I had to find out if I'm even cut out for rescue work.

Chapter Sixteen

MY RESEARCH

I learned that "Pit Bull" is a slang term that refers to the American Pit Bull Terrier, the American Staffordshire Terrier, and the Staffordshire Bull Terrier. All three of these breeds are considered pit bulls and/or bully breeds as well as any dog with similar physical appearances.

I learned that in the nineteenth century, they were referred to as "The nanny dogs" because of their love and tolerance for children. I learned about "Sergeant Stubby," the most decorated war dog during World War I. Today, pit bulls and pit bull types are banned from military bases.

In the early 1900s, pit bulls were considered "The Spirit of America." They are the only breed to have ever been on the cover of *Life* magazine three times.

Pit bulls are intelligent and easily trained. They are strong, athletic, and agile. They are determined and very eager to please. They are also good family dogs. Any breed, if not bred well, exercised, socialized, trained, and treated with love and respect, can have behavior problems. The same can be said about people too. Pit bulls aren't any more problematic than any other breed by nature.

I also learned about the unthinkable and unspeakable torment and torture that pit bulls have endured from scumbags who wanted them to fight. If any human being endured the same treatment, they would be fighting mad too.

Their strength, tenacity, and athleticism appeal to people with bad intentions. These are twisted people who get pit bulls and train them to fight. They start when puppies are just weeks old. In one way, they scruff the necks of two puppies and repeatedly push them into each other's face to encourage aggression. I'll say it again: this kind of treatment would make any of us aggressive. This is just one of their twisted techniques. There are many, and they are all torturous.

Pit bulls are not inherently aggressive. Many of them suffer at the hands of irresponsible owners drawn to the dog's macho image, probably because of what they are lacking in themselves that the pit bull makes up for.

I feel that there are way too many of the wrong people—irresponsible people—who own pit bulls. These people are the ones who are, in fact, ruining their reputation.

The media is hurting their reputation too. They are infamous for over-reporting, misreporting, and even not reporting the whole story. If a pit bull bites, mauls, or attacks, the media will often say that it was a pit bull. If any other breed of dog bites, mauls, or attacks, the media doesn't specify the breed. If there is a story about a pit bull that has done a heroic act, they simply report it as a heroic dog.

Nowadays, many states, counties, and municipal governments are turning to Breed Specific Legislation (BSL) that targets specific breeds as an answer to dog attacks.

BSL is the banning or restriction of specific breeds of dogs considered "dangerous" such as the pit bull, Rottweiler, Doberman Pincher, Chow Chow, and German Shepherd. In my opinion, pit bulls and pit bull–type dogs are the target of these laws. Never in history has any other dog breed suffered the same kind of discrimination, judgment, ridicule, prejudice, and abuse as the Pit Bull Terrier. It is very clear to me that we need to stop blaming the dogs and start blaming the real culprits: people. Pit bulls are not vicious villains. They are innocent victims. This is why I fight for them, speak for them, and rescue them.

In Denver, Colorado, where the BSL was enforced, officers knocked on doors of people living with their pet pit bulls and pit bull types. They seized these dogs to later kill them. This was legal for authorities to do. It was reported that over 3,000 dogs were killed for no other reason other than being a pit bull or the like. Many of these seized dogs didn't even have any pit bull bloodline in them but had some of the same physical features.

After working at the shelters, I became aware of the fact that what I see in a mixed breed dog is, almost always, not the same as what somebody else sees. It seems that everybody sees something different. There are a lot of different breeds that have short hair coats, wide heads, short muzzles, muscular bodies, and some with cropped ears that resemble pit bulls. The Boxer for example is often mistaken for a pit bull. So what I'd like to know is what qualifies an individual to be an expert on mixed breed dogs by only looking at them when the only way to know for sure is by DNA.

I cannot imagine what that had to be like for the owners of those dogs. I think the authorities would have to kill me first, although it's easy for me to say that. Nevertheless, I simply cannot imagine.

Chapter Seventeen

NO MATTER WHAT

I remember one day when I was super stressed and feeling hopeless and helpless. I felt defeated. I had so much pent up anxiety from rescuing. I had to let it go so I wrote down what I was feeling and saved it—although, I'm not sure why I saved it. Maybe God wanted me too so I could put it in my book that I didn't even know I would be writing one day.

"I just cannot do this anymore. There's too many pit bulls that are needing help, but I am one person doing the best that I can. I want to throw in the towel. I think I've done my share, but I think I'm losing this fight."

Then, I'd come face to face again with another pit bull in dire need, and so, I continue my fight to save them.

On another day while I was feeling so much sympathy for pit bulls, I wrote them a letter…

Dear Pit Bull,

I, for one, know that people have so unfairly given you the bad reputation that you have and all because of the things that they forced you to do, the abuse and neglect that they inflicted upon you. It weighs so heavy on my heart, and for this, I am making this commitment to you...

To all of you who suffered physically and emotionally or have been killed because of people's ignorance, insecurities, and greed, I am truly sorry. I promise that, no matter what, I will rescue you, fight for you, and lay down and die for you if that's what I have to do to save you. I promise that I will do this each and every day for the rest of my life. Why...? Because I know in my heart of hearts that you would do the same for me too. No matter what, I will always love you.

Connie Bowman, 2003

Five years later, I hear about the NFL football player, whose name I refuse to write in my book, whose name I cannot even say without spitting fire, had just been busted for operating and participating in dog fights.

I cannot even express how I felt then, and still feel now, but I can say this: I hate him, I hate his buddies, and I hate anybody that has anything to do with dogfighting, nor can I or will I forgive them. And, this I put mildly. I also hate the NFL for allowing him to play again.

Not too long ago, there was a story that went viral when somebody videotaped, while at a professional soccer game in Argentina, a dog that had wandered onto the soccer field. One of the players picked the dog up with both hands around the neck and slammed the dog into a chain link fence. The player was kicked off of the soccer league permanently. I cannot understand why this NFL player is allowed to play football again.

When the story first broke, I was happy to hear that Nike Co. had dropped him like a hot potato; so happy, that I named one of my rescued puppies, "Nike." However, Nike Co. has since endorsed him again.

I think his punishment was an insult. First of all, he was quoted in *The Atlanta Journal-Constitution*: "I'm never at the house...I left the house with my family members and my cousin...They just haven't been doing the right thing...It's unfortunate I have to take the heat behind it. If I'm not there, I don't know what's going on." According to *The Virginian-Pilot* newspaper, he also said at that time, "It's a call for me to really tighten down on who I'm trying to take care of.... Lesson learned for me." All was proven in a court of law that he was lying.

In 2012 on a NFL website he was quoted, "I knew how to lie with a straight face. I knew I was going to try to lie my way through the whole dogfighting case and see if money, good lawyers, and manipulating the system could get me out of the position I was in—which was a terrible position."

He tortured those dogs. He had strategically chained them to car axels with enough room to come nose to nose with the other dogs, but not make contact. He shot dogs, hung dogs, drowned dogs by putting their heads in a five gallon bucket of water. One dog was repeatedly lifted over his and his partners' heads and slammed into the concrete until the poor dog was dead. He electrocuted dogs by attaching car battery cables to a car battery and the other end to their ears and throwing them into a pool. It was reported that there were scratches on the sides of the pool where the dogs must have been desperately tried to claw their way out of the pool. He also took the family dog and put it in the pit with fighting dogs. It was reported by an eyewitness that he laughed as the fighting dogs tore it to pieces. But today, he is allowed to own a dog. How is this even possible? As far as I'm concerned, he just gave all of us animal advocates, a cold slap in the face and probably laughed about that too. Read it again if you have too. I did not make this stuff up. It was reported by an eyewitness. Again, I cannot express what I am feeling right at this moment.

After plea bargaining, he wasn't even charged with animal cruelty even though he at first lied about abusing and/or killing any of the dogs. Only after he failed a lie detector test and was backed into a corner while learning that his co-defendants had told on him, did he admit to killing two dogs; but, he in fact killed more than two. People say that he did his time. I say he did not. He plea bargained. I don't believe he is sorry, maybe only for getting caught. He has never shown remorse nor has he ever come to face any of the dogs since they started their rehabilitation. Some of the dogs, even six years later, still display the trauma they once endured. And, let us not forget about Georgia, whose teeth were pulled so she couldn't bite the stud dogs when she had been placed in a rape stand time and time again. Did you get that? A rape stand: a contraption made to hold a female dog securely so male dogs can mount her. Yes, she was raped. I so wish the law would be an eye for an eye, that way he truly would have paid his debt. He would've suffered the consequences.

About three years after the story broke, I was in a store looking for a book, when I looked up, and right in front of my face was his autobiography. I was stunned that not only does he continue to make money playing football, but now he's going to make money off of his pathetic autobiography. Thinking how some of the dogs are still severely traumatized—while he continues to make millions of dollars—made my blood boil. I lost control of myself and stole one of his books. Now I know the money he lost making on this one book won't hurt his pocket in the least but that's one book he won't make money on. I took the stinking book home and shredded it by hand, page by page. Somehow it made me feel like I got one in for all of his innocent victims—and that made me feel really good.

I always try to find the positive in every negative, including this. The positive that came out of all this is a new light was shed on the fact that dogfighting is real. It's barbaric, and it's happening everywhere. Finally, the dogs were rescued from living in hell, and their torture was over.

For the first time in history, the lives of these fighting dogs were spared, and they were given a second chance at a life that they so deserve. They opened the door for all fighting dogs to be given a second chance as well. They proved to the world that they are only the reflection of the monsters that owned them, not monsters themselves. Their rehabilitation should've spoke volumes to all anti-pit bull people. If anybody raised their child in the same way these dogs were raised, there is no doubt in my mind that the child would behave the same.

I am so proud of all of them. They have been rehabilitated, they are thriving and are true ambassadors of their breed. Some are service dogs.

Some are therapy dogs. Some are even helping children to overcome their fear of reading out loud by simply listening to the children read to them. And I pray that God blesses those dogs in a mighty way.

I shed a lot of tears for those poor innocent babies and still do sometimes. I so desperately wanted to hold them, love them, and tell them that they were safe now as I do with my rescued dogs. I believe God gave me that opportunity, because two years ago, I actually met one of the dogs rescued from the evil football player when I went to Best Friends Animal Sanctuary in Utah to volunteer. Her name was Ellen.

When I first laid eyes on her, my heart shattered by all the physical scars she had. I wanted to just cry my heart out to her with apologies, but somehow I was able to keep my emotions from overflowing because I didn't want her to feed off of them. I kept telling myself over and over to think happy thoughts.

I read stories to her and sang songs to her too. I was able to touch her and love her—and she loved me back by giving me kisses. I got to teach her the down command without bribing her with food to help her pass her C.G.C. test. I spent most of my time there with Ellen. When it was time for me to leave, I promised her that I would come back to see her again. Only this time when I do go back to Best Friends, I will visit Ellen where she was laid to rest in Best Friends Angel's Rest. She passed away just last year. Although it broke my heart to hear the news, I have peace knowing that she was finally loved.

Meeting Ellen was the biggest honor I have ever had. "I will keep you in my heart forever sweet girl."

Chapter Eighteen

HOMECOMING

Babe was the only dog in the house during the four days the other dogs were hospitalized, and I have to say it was rather nice and quiet. I noticed my stress level had decreased, and I wasn't feeling tense from having to be so careful and cautious all the time with the dogs. This got me to thinking about how hard I tried to prevent any dog fights—and the fear and stress of it all had most likely contributed to the fight. The dogs picked up on it.

Breeze taught me that I'm not qualified to have so many dogs at the same time, and I promised her that I would not have so many anymore. My plan was once I was down to two dogs, I wouldn't add any more. However, I still have a need to rescue, which I would still do, only one dog at a time. Then when one dog gets adopted, that will open the door for another dog to be rescued.

Dr. A. released Breeze and Spot from the hospital, but I still wasn't ready for them to come home. I was still afraid. My vet bill was already in the thousands of dollars, and if they stayed even one more day, it would seem to skyrocket into the millions. I can feel the tension building again.

I took Breeze, and John took Spot when we went home. I put Spot in our room, and Breeze in the office. I didn't want Babe and Breeze together yet because of all the wounds and drain tubes on Breeze. She might accidentally get hurt. But, I should've known better. Babe would probably be a great comfort for her as he always was with me. It was breaking my heart to keep them separated. Breeze would lay by the doors inside the office, and Babe would lay by the doors outside the office—and both of them would cry for each other. On the second day, I let them together, and Babe did exactly what I thought he'd do. He gave her comfort and TLC that only Babe can give.

I had a private cremation for Frank so I could have his cremains to bury. I chose a place in one corner of the backyard where there are two large palm trees with a giant red rock in between. I buried him right beneath the red rock. Sonya bought me a headstone with an inscription that says:

> *If tears could build a highway*
> *And memories a lane,*
> *I'd walk right up to Heaven*
> *And bring you home again.*

Frank will always be with me.

Breeze and Spot healed nicely. I felt bad for Spot because he was singled out, but that's just the way it had to be.

While at work, I was talking to one of the animal control officers who said he used to train dogs at one time. I told him about my situation with my dogs and asked him if thought there was a way that Breeze and Spot could ever live in harmony. He suggested that I muzzle both of them and let them go at it. They wouldn't get hurt because of the muzzles, and they would end up wearing each other out and think there would be no use in fighting. Just the word, "Muzzle" made me cringe.

I don't know why at that time but what the AC officer was telling me had made sense and even gave me hope; however, while I am writing these words, it makes no sense to me now.

In spite of this, and after a few more attempts of Breeze trying to attack Spot, I thought maybe it would be worth trying. Of course, I thought wrong. Breeze slipped out of the muzzle and did some pretty serious injuries on Spot and back to the hospital he went.

If that wasn't stupid enough, several months after that, I woke up very early one morning to use the bathroom. Still not completely awake, on my way back to bed, I forgot that Spot and I slept in the spare bedroom that night. When Breeze came over to greet me, I put her in the spare bedroom and closed the door. Within seconds, I could hear that blood curdling, dreadful growling of a fight in progress. *Oh my gosh...what did I just do?* I felt that I purposely put Breeze in a fighting pit. I opened the door and somehow managed to get Breeze out and then close the door again—but not soon enough for she was torn up again. I knew that Spot probably was too.

Once again, we went to the hospital, I took Breeze and John took Spot. I was so mad at myself. *How could I be so stupid, what is wrong with me?* I couldn't handle it anymore. We had already paid out over seven thousand dollars in vet bills. And...while my emotions were overflowing, I quickly made a decision to let Breeze go to sleep. Even several years later, I still don't know if it was the right decision. But I do know it was a decision I should've never tried to make while I was such an emotional wreck.

Today, I can confidently say that none of this was Breeze's fault. It was all my fault. The solution to all of this was very simple if I just would've continued training Breeze as well as Spot. I don't know if they would've ever been able to live in harmony, but I am quite sure that I would've had better control. Now, because of my stupidity, two of my dogs had to die. I hate myself for being so stupid, and I don't know if I will ever be able to forgive myself. Actually, there would be no point in doing so…the damage is done. My dogs are dead.

I was so full of anger for a very long time. I hated the world and everybody in it, but most of all, I hated myself.

> *To my Serenity Breeze,*
> *How can you ever forgive me? What I couldn't see when you were with me, it's all so very clear to me now. I'm so sorry that I hurt you. I live with it every day. And all the pain that I put you through…I wish that I could take it all away and be the one who catches all your tears. I never saw your sorrow in all the years we were together. You are always and forever in my heart. I love and miss you so very much.*

I buried Breeze with Frank under the big red rock between the two palm trees. They will always be with me.

My heart would break every time I'd look at Babe. He was lost without his Breeze for he loved her so much. Sometimes, I think he thought he'd hear her and then would go looking around the house for her. Sometimes, I think I would hear her too.

Within three years, I had to let two of my dogs go to sleep, and with Babe pushing fifteen years, I worry about the time I had left with him. I also lost a pit bull that I was very close to, Jonah. She was not mine nor was she one of my rescues, but I loved her just the same. Matter of fact, Jonah rescued me one day from being attacked by yet another human. She was very sweet and so beautiful. Jonah was only four years old when she just suddenly and mysteriously died. She will always be in my heart.

Chapter Nineteen

JOSEPHINA

I was still grieving my loss of Frank and Breeze when my son Anthony surprised me.

I had mentioned to him one day that I would like to have another white pit bull but had completely forgotten about it. My Anthony never forgot. For my birthday he gave me a white pit bull puppy, and she was just what I needed. She got me out of my head where I was mentally beating myself up. She was therapeutic for me, and the best anti-depressant in the world. I named her Josephina aka Josie.

I still had to tell John that I had a new puppy. I was sure he was not going to be happy about it. If I told him that she was a birthday present from Anthony, I was afraid it would be too easy for him to tell Anthony to take her back, but if I told him that I found her, it would buy some time for him to fall in love with her. And that was my story. I told him I found her on the street heading towards the busy highway, and she almost got hit by a car right in front of me.

"What was I to do" I asked. "You know I can never pass by a stray animal and not try to help."

John was very familiar with the steps I take to reunite a lost animal with its owner so he countered with, "Well then, you better get her scanned for a microchip and get busy on the computer placing found ads, checking lost and found, make some found flyers, run an ad in the newspaper, etc."

The next day when he came home from work he said, "Did you find her owner?"

"No."

"Did you put an ad in the newspaper?"

"Yes"

Then he said, "I looked in the paper and didn't see it."

I remember thinking that I had just been caught, but I said, "It will probably be in tomorrow's paper." That was our conversation for the next few days till I couldn't take deceiving him anymore and I told him the truth. He knew I was lying. Although he wasn't happy about it, he wasn't mad either—and I knew that I could keep her.

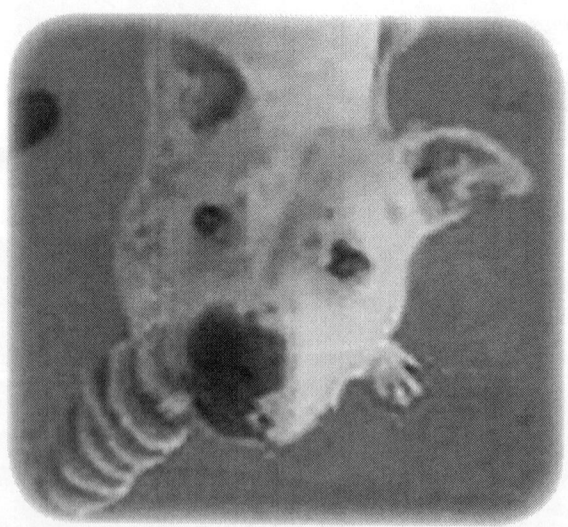

I still have my Josephina. She has been a good girl and has always been such a happy dog with a really cute personality. I put an empty cookie box on the floor in the kitchen to take out with the trash. Josie was sniffing around the box, but I didn't think much of it. A little while later, I realized I hadn't seen her for a short time so I went looking to see what she was doing. I found her sitting in the middle of the backyard with the cookie box stuck on her head. She didn't panic or even try to get it off. She was just sitting quietly. I wish I would've gotten a picture. I would've like to see how see managed to get the box on her head and then go from the kitchen, through the doggy door, and out to the backyard. I so glad it wasn't a peanut butter jar. Another time when she was still a puppy and chewing things up, she took a cushion off of the couch and tried to pull it through the doggy door...but it got stuck which left her stuck outside. We weren't at home so I don't know how long she was out there. John found her when he got home and said she was standing at the back door with a huge smile on her face, wagging her whole body. I can imagine her on the outside of the doggy door pulling with all her might to get that cushion through.

Josie has helped me tremendously with the rescued dogs that came after her, which happened to be four puppies from four different rescues. Josie had never had a litter of her own, but she still had maternal instincts. It was very heartwarming to watch her nurture the little ones as if she were their mother.

The first puppy of the four that I rescued was only three weeks old.

Chapter Twenty

LITTLE BITTY BUGGA BOO

One of my neighbors came to me asking for help with a pit bull puppy that he got the night before. He said the puppy wouldn't stop crying and couldn't get the puppy to eat. I went to my neighbor's house to see the puppy and what I could do, if anything. I was shocked when he brought out a tiny little baby that, to me, was clearly only a couple of weeks old, much too young to be away from its mother and littermates. My neighbor told me he got the puppy from some guy standing on a street corner waving puppies in his hands at traffic and saying, "Free puppies."

I explained to him that the puppy was too young to have left his mother and that's probably why he won't stop crying. He asked me how to bottle feed a puppy, then showed me a regular baby bottle filled with whole milk that he was trying to feed him. I knew then that I should ask him if I could take the puppy, but I didn't. I tried to explain to him that another reason the puppy is crying is because he's hungry, but he shouldn't try to feed the puppy whole milk. I started to tell him to go to the pet food store and get puppy bottles and puppy formula when he asked me if I would take the puppy. I told him that if I brought another dog into my house that John would probably throw me out even though I knew John wouldn't do that. I told him to go to the pet food store, and I would help feed the puppy and help him with whatever else I could do.

Once we got the puppy fed, the little guy quieted right down and fell asleep. I wanted to take him home with me, and as I walked away, it weighed so heavily on my heart. I told myself that I would check on them first thing in the morning.

When John came home from work, I casually mentioned the neighbor and his puppy. I told him it was too young to be away from its mother and wasn't eating...and our neighbor didn't know what to do.

"Why didn't you bring him home? You better go get that baby and bring him home," John said.

My husband is a true saint.

I ran across the street to my neighbor's house and asked him if he still wanted me to take the puppy...and he said yes. Instantly, the heaviness in my heart had gone away.

After working at the kill shelter for a few years, I ended up emotionally drained and had to quit. From there, I went to work at an actual no kill shelter for a couple of years but then got fired for insubordination. In spite of the fact that it was a no kill shelter, they rarely ever took in pit bulls, like their lives were not worth saving. Every time I had to turn one away, I would be livid until I finally blew my stack and got fired for it.

And from there, I went to work at another animal hospital. I took the little guy to work with me, and one of the vets that I worked for examined him. She told me that he was approximately three weeks old. Dr. H. gave me a recipe that's made with goat's milk to feed the little guy. He ate like there was no tomorrow, the poor thing had been starving. He had a nice round fat belly when he was done eating and then fell right to sleep.

Dr. G. ran the hospital and told me it would be okay if I brought the little guy to work with me every day, and by doing that, we could display him in the reception area to promote his adoption when he was old enough to be adopted. I loved going to work with him but that meant that we were together all day, every day. I was quickly getting attached.

I didn't want to name him but had to call him something. One day we were in the backyard sitting on the grass when I noticed that the grass was taller than he was. He reminded me of a little bug in the grass. And with that, he was named, "Little Bug," short for "Little Bitty Bugga Boo." Little Bug stole my heart. Nevertheless, I had to remember my promise to Breeze: I knew I would have to find him a home.

The first thing we did every morning was go outside so Bug could relieve himself. I'd tell him, "Let's go do a pee" and as soon as he'd pee, I made it a big celebration. With that and Josie's help teaching Bug to use the doggy door, he was not only house broke in record time but was also peeing on command.

Bug was growing fast and so was my love for him. He was becoming a sweet and loving little soul that blessed my heart every day.

He loved going to work and his daily routine when we got there was to first walk me over to the long stretch of grassy area to do a pee which seemed to always be at one end or the other, never in the middle of the grass. He would do his pee, then look up at me out of the corner of his eye as if he were saying to me, "Are you ready?" Then, he would run all the way to the other end of the grass, around the corner of the building, past the front doors, and stop at the door to the employee's entrance tugging me behind on the other end of the leash. He'd wait for me to open the door and take off running again down the hall to the doctor's office where he'd practically jump into Dr. G's and Dr. H's arms. After saying good morning to them, he'd quickly run further down the hall to the treatment room where the vet technicians and the kennel employees were to tell them good morning and then into the reception area to do the same. He then had about fifteen minutes of play time. When it was time to open the doors for business, he'd go into his kennel and fall fast asleep.

When Bug was old enough, I had him neutered, vaccinated, micro chipped, and then put him up for adoption. In my mind, I battled with putting him up for adoption because I was so attached to him and wanted to keep him, but I wanted to keep my promise to Breeze just as much.

I put together a pre-adoption screening application complete with trick questions to help me with deciding on who would be the best candidate in adopting Bug—and I planned on doing home checks. The application turned out to be more like an interrogation, but I had to be sure in finding Bug the best home. Although in my mind and in my heart, I knew he was already in the best home he could be.

Everybody that met Bug fell in love with him, but most people already had a dog or two. They didn't want another and that was okay with me. For those that were interested in adopting him, I immediately started sizing them up. I had to find something that would disqualify them. Something like, the potential adopter didn't earn over one hundred thousand dollars a year…sorry, you've been disqualified. Or, the potential adopter was not a college graduate…sorry, you've been disqualified. If they were left handed instead of right handed, disqualified. If I didn't like the car they drove, disqualified. There is nobody good enough for my Little Bug. I desperately wanted to keep him. I was sabotaging his adoption and knew it. I disqualified at least twenty five applicants. The longer I did that, the longer I could keep him.

Suddenly, I'd remember my Breeze. I had to keep my promise. I was so torn. I wanted to do what was right. I still had three other dogs at home. I think I already broke my promise because I was keeping those three.

So, what's one more if you already broke your promise? You might as well keep Bug.

No, don't be stupid, you can't keep Bug. Breeze died because you were stupid.

It was like having the devil on one shoulder and an angel on the other shoulder telling me what to do. I battled with this every day. I had to let Bug go.

A young couple called me inquiring about Bug. I told them to meet me at the animal hospital where they could meet Bug. They said they already had a small dog. I told them to bring their dog too.

When they arrived, I talked with them for a little while and met their little dog. They seemed to be the best candidate's so far, and I was feeling pretty good about them. I brought Bug outside for them to meet—and they fell in love. There was an instant connection with all of them.

I had them fill out my interrogation form, and after looking it over, I only had two concerns. My first concern was that he was in the military. I know that bully breeds have been banned from military bases. In my mind, I disqualified them. But then, they said they don't live on the base, and they just bought a brand new home.

Darn.

My other concern was they were a young couple without kids but planned on having kids in the future. I learned, while working at the shelters, that this is one of the top five reasons that people dump their dogs at a shelter. Specifically, "We're having a baby." I always thought to myself, "So what, the dog was there first." So, I mentally disqualified them again.

One of the questions on my application is, "If you plan on having kids in the future, will you keep your commitment to this dog?" They answered, "Yes, the dog is family too."

Double darn.

I decided to let the couple take Bug for a trial run for a few days to see if Bug is what they were wanting. At the same time I would be secretly trying to sabotage the adoption. After a few days, they wanted to adopt Bug even more than ever. After doing a home check, I found nothing wrong. I had to stop playing this insane game. I had to let them adopt Bug, but with the understanding that if for whatever reason it does not work out, they have to give him back to me. They agreed, and my Little Bitty Bugga Boo went to his new home. I cried. I don't know if I cried happy tears or sad tears—but I cried.

Chapter Twenty One

LORD HAVE MERCY

One day while I was at work, a young woman came in and asked my co-worker if she knew of any Veterinarians that were pit bull friendly. I thought it was a strange question and got my attention so I told the woman that the doctors here are pit bull friendly—and one of them even has a pit bull. She went on to tell me that she and her uncle live with their grandmother and that her uncle has three pit bulls that he physically beats every day. It felt like I had just been punched in the stomach. I introduced myself to her and told her that I rescue pit bulls. She said her name was, "Mercy," and she and her grandmother didn't know what to do. I told her if she wasn't willing to give me his name and address, I didn't want to hear anymore. It is unbearable for me to know that an animal is being abused, and I can't do anything to help. Mercy wrote his name and address on a piece of paper and gave it to me. She also said that her uncle had a warrant for his arrest. She gave me her phone number and asked if I could help save the dogs. I still had four hours before I got off work, but I told her I would call her then.

For the next four hours, all I could do was think about those poor babies getting beat and the more I thought about it, the madder I got—and the madder I got, the harder it was for me to think clearly. I had to come up with a plan. I didn't know what I was walking into, but I knew that, do or die, I was going to get those dogs.

I called Mercy when I got off work and she told that her grandma was so happy I was coming to rescue the dogs. She said grandma was in tears of joy. Mercy said that her uncle wasn't home at that time, and she gave me directions to her grandma's house. I decided to call a couple of friends to help me out because there were three dogs that we were going to be rescued.

I decided to go home to change my clothes first and started thinking that Mercy said her uncle had a warrant for his arrest so I thought that I would wear my t-shirt that says, "L.V.M.P.D. K-9 Unit." If he happened to be there, it just might influence him to surrender the dogs. I met my friends down the street from grandmas and called Mercy again to see if the uncle had come back—and if now was a good time to get the dogs. First Mercy said that she and grandma were so excited and that now would be a good time. I told her we were going to get the dogs and leave right away. I would call her afterwards, and she said okay.

We drove up to grandma's house. I opened the back of my SUV and grabbed three leashes for each one of us. We ran up to the door where Mercy and Grandma were waiting for us with the dogs. We leashed up each dog, ran to my truck put them in, shut the door, and were gone. It went very fast and smooth without any problems at all. Except now, I didn't know what to do with these three dogs nor where to take them. At least they were safe. While driving around trying to figure out if I should just take them to my house or find someplace else, my phone rings. I remembered I was supposed to call Mercy. I answered and it was grandma. She was crying. I thought she was crying because the rescue was a success and she was happy, but I was wrong. Grandma wasn't happy at all.

She was crying and asking, "Why did you take my babies away from me. They didn't do anything wrong. Why did you take them?"

"Wait a minute, what did you just say? I thought you knew we were coming. Isn't that what you wanted, for the dogs to get rescued from being abused?"

"No, my babies are not abused, they sleep in my bed with me. I love my babies. Who told you they were abused?"

"Mercy."

"Oh my goodness, what did Mercy tell you?"

I told her everything from the very beginning, and Grandma said, "I don't know how to tell you this, but my granddaughter Mercy is very mentally ill. She won't take her medication, and this is what happens."

Grandma said that the state had even taken Mercy's children because she is so unstable without her meds. She also said that there isn't even an uncle—it's just Grandma and Mercy.

Oh my gosh, is this really happening?

Grandma said she had no clue about what was happening. That Mercy never mentioned to her that we were coming to take the dogs. She said that Mercy had told her to come to the door to look at something and that's when we rushed in and stole Grandma's dogs.

"It all happened so fast, I didn't know what to say."

I was so embarrassed, I didn't know what to say. After talking to Grandma on the phone for about thirty minutes, I asked her if she wanted me to bring her dogs back.

"Oh please, please bring my babies back to me. You can come into my house, and you will see they are not being abused."

I went back to Grandma's and gave back her dogs. They were overjoyed to be back home. Grandma was crying again, but this time, they really were tears of joy.

Chapter Twenty Two

WHY HAVE A DOG?

When I first started rescuing pit bulls, I had some simple business cards with my name and phone number made with my slogan, "A friend indeed for a pit bull in need." I'd hand them out to anybody that had a pit bull, knew somebody that had a pit bull, or simply said, pit bull. It didn't take long for my phone to start ringing. Most of the time it would be somebody wanting me to take their dog that they could no longer keep for whatever lame reason. Then, I'd get calls that were more urgent.

I had not changed into my rescue tights and cape with the capital R on my chest for a while—and I wasn't sure if it would still fit—when I got a call about an abused and neglected pit bull in somebody's backyard with no shelter from the blazing sun of over one hundred degrees. I made sure it fit.

The caller told me that he lived next door to the dog's owner who had been physically abusive to the dog. He also said that he had never in two years seen the dog outside of the backyard nor had he ever seen any kind of shelter for the dog. He said he finally convinced the owner to give the dog up, but he couldn't find a rescue that had room for the dog.

I met the caller at his house, and he let me look over the wall to where the dog was. There, in fact, wasn't any shelter from the blazing sun nor was there any water. I asked if the owner was at home, and he said no. I asked if the dog was friendly, and he said yes. I went to my car, got a leash, and went to the gate where the dog was. I could see his back side was blistered. I could feel my blood boiling, and at that point, I knew I was taking the dog no matter what or who would try to get in my way. I put a leash on him, opened the gate, and got him in my car. I took him to Dr. H who confirmed that the dog had been sunburned. Dr. H also said that there was a lot of scar tissue that could be indicative of being sunburned before. She gave me ointment and antibiotics but said the scar tissue was probably permanent.

This dog went from never leaving his backyard for two years to going on the road with his adopter who is a trucker. He was named, "Roadie."

Another time, I got a call one day from somebody who said their neighbor had a pit bull that was constantly barking and crying. They said they rarely ever saw anybody with the dog, and the few times they did see somebody, they were telling the dog to shut up.

I knew what the problem was right away. The poor dog was bored and lonely—and desperately trying to get somebody's attention. The caller said they reported it to animal control twice, but nothing was done. I felt I should go check it out so I asked for the address. When I got there, I could hear the dog barking and crying so I went to the gate and called the dog. He ran to the gate wiggling his whole body. He seemed to be happy that he finally got somebody's attention. I petted him and talked to him for a little while, and then I thought I'd knock on the door and maybe talk to the owner. When I walked away, the dog cried and then started howling. My heart was busting over this poor dog that was so lonely.

The owner opened the front door. I introduced myself and told him one of his neighbors called me because of his dog barking. I came over to offer him my help. I tried to explain that the reason the dog was barking and crying all the time was because he was lonely and bored. I said dogs are pack animals, and when they are singled out like this, they become scared and insecure.

"Your dog is trying to get your attention." I started to ask him if he would allow his dog to come in the house.

He looked directly into my eyes and said, "There's nothing wrong with my dog, and you need to mind your own business."

Chills ran down my spine, but I wasn't giving up. I said, "I'd be more than happy to come over and take your dog for a walk a couple times a week"

He then walked into the house and slammed the door.

I really hate it when people tell me to mind my own business because dogs are my business. When they tell me to mind my own business, it just fuels my fire. Whether I'm right or wrong, it doesn't matter to me. What does matter is the dog. I know there's always a possibility that I could get hurt doing a rescue—or even get arrested—but it doesn't stop me. I wouldn't care as long as the dog got to safety. I am willing to pay the consequences when I know the dog is safe. Call me crazy. I never claimed that I wasn't.

I stopped by the gate again and told the dog that I would be back. As I was leaving, he started crying again, and as I drove away, I started crying. I don't understand why people get dogs and leave them in the backyard with no human interaction or contact—and sometimes, with little food and water. I would be barking my but off too.

I have come to find that there are, "People" and there are, "Animal People." Neither understands the other. Personally, I don't like, "People."

I went back to the house a couple more times and tried to talk to the owner. I practically begged him to at least let me take the dog for walks, but I got the same response. He'd slam the door in my face. After a couple of months of this, I'm feeling that I tried to do the right thing by talking to the owner, but it didn't work so I started thinking that I'm going to have to take his dog. But, there has to be another way. Then I get another call from the same person who first told me about the dog, only this time she said she thinks he was beating the dog. She said she heard him yelling at the dog to shut up, and then she heard the dog yelping. Now I knew I was going to take his dog. I went to the house the next day and called the dog over to the gate. This time he was very timid. I told myself I am going to try one more time to talk some sense into this guy's head, and I knocked on the door. There was no answer so I took that as a sign that it was time to take the dog. I opened the back of my truck, got a leash, went to the gate, and opened it. I slipped the leash over the dog's head. He was still very timid, and I wondered what the owner did to this poor baby. A neighbor came outside and was watching me so I told the neighbor that I was with the humane society. It was the only thing I could think of. The dog was very apprehensive to walk through the gate, but I encouraged him with some lunch meat. I quickly got him to my truck and was getting ready to load him in. Somehow I dropped the leash. The dog got spooked and ran back into his backyard.

The owner then came outside and said, "What do you think you're doing?"

I had to think fast and all I could come up with was, "You are in violation, and either I take this dog or you will be cited by animal control who are on their way as we speak."

He grabbed my leash off of his dog and threw it at me and said, "Get the hell off of my property."

Not knowing when to stop, I said, "Have it your way."

And I left. I was shaking and scared for the dog. I prayed he wouldn't take this out on him. I then called animal control and told them about the dog being abused. They said they would send somebody out. I waited down the street where I couldn't be seen—but nobody came. I asked the woman who originally called me to keep her eyes opened for animal control and then let me know. I called her the next day, but she said she never saw them. I had to stand with my arms out as if I were holding that baby in my arms, and I had to give him to God.

I prayed for that dog's safety every day for two weeks, and then the same woman called me and said, "The dog has been laying in the same position for two days now. I think he's dead."

I felt like I had been ran over by a train. I called animal control again. This time they actually sent somebody to the house, but it was too late.

Chapter Twenty Three

BOBO BOWMAN

Shortly after Bug was adopted, a lady contacted me to ask if I could take her eight week old pit bull puppy because she could no longer keep him. She said the reason why she took him in the first place was because somebody was selling puppies at a local store and he was the last one left. She felt sorry for him. She paid fifty dollars for him. When she took him for a checkup, the doctor told her the puppy was full of parasites, and she **ended** up paying even more money for a puppy that she never really wanted.

She said if she couldn't find anybody to take him, she was going to take him to the shelter, that was pretty much all she had to say to me. I knew I had to rescue the puppy. Knowing that the no kill shelters are always maxed out, if she did take him to a shelter, it would be the kill shelter. I told her I wanted to talk to my husband and would call her back.

I knew we were going to take the puppy, but what I didn't know was that John was going to pay the lady the fifty dollars that she originally spent to get the puppy. John said, "It's the holidays. They have kids and probably need the money." I was so proud of my husband. We laugh about it today because we paid fifty dollars to rescue a puppy.

This little guy had the biggest paws I had ever seen on a puppy. He hardly had any fur, and with it being winter, I had to keep him warm. I found a little camouflaged thermo shirt at the pet supply store that did the trick. He was a black and white puppy with white socks. I thought if his big paws were black, he'd look like a soldier with his camouflaged shirt on.

It was fun to have a puppy in the house again, and this guy stole John's heart this time. I knew John was going to want to keep him. I was trying to keep my promise to Breeze, and if we didn't keep Little Bug, we're not keeping this little one.

"You want to keep this puppy don't you?" I would ask John.

"Yes, look at him. Don't you want to keep him?"

I'd quickly say, "No... I don't know."

We went back and forth with this for several days until I justified it with, "It is the holidays, and John's birthday is New Year's Eve." I guess this is where I'm supposed to say, "Merry Christmas and Happy Birthday Babe."

We were trying to think of a name for the pup when a friend of ours said, "How about Bobo?" John then said, "Bobo Bowman, it has a nice ring to it." And, Bobo Bowman it was.

When Bobo was old enough, I had him vaccinated, micro chipped, and neutered. Before surgery, we found out that little Bobo had cryptorchidism, which means that one of his testicles had not descended so Dr. H. had to make two incisions into his abdomen to find the testicle that had not descended and remove it too. This was a more difficult surgery than the typical neuter surgery where animals are dropped off in the mornings to be sterilized and picked up that same afternoon. Bobo had to stay a couple of nights. The doctor told me that he was doing fine but was very cold so they put socks on his paws...but had a hard time finding socks big enough for his huge paws.

Bobo was a very mellow puppy and took sleeping very seriously. I swear this puppy had narcolepsy because within seconds he would fall into a deep sleep. One second he was playing and the very next second he was snoring. It was the funniest thing to see. There was no waking Bobo; a light sleeper, he was not.

With Babe being close to fifteen years old, I worried that Bobo would be too much for him, but Babe always loved puppies and loved Bobo too. Wherever Babe was, so was Bobo. I mentioned to John that I could see Babe was slowing down, and we should try to mentally prepare ourselves for when it's time to let him go. John said, "It's not time, he'll be okay." I hoped he was right.

Just a couple of months later, I got up very early one morning while John was getting ready to go out of town on business. He looked at me and said, "It's time."

Still half asleep I said, "Time for what?"

"Baby Boy, he can't get up."

I became fully awake at that point and remember saying, "Noooo, not now, not my Baby Boy."

John told me to look at him, but I couldn't. I couldn't stop crying. Babe was always so in tune with my emotions that I didn't want to stress him out. I kept telling myself to get a grip. When I did, I laid down with Babe and just held on to him like I was never going to let him go. I talked to him and told him that he is the best dog in the whole-wide world. With tears running down my face, I told him how much I loved him and will always love him. Just like Babe always did in the past when I was crying, he licked my tears. That's when I completely lost my grip and started crying my eyes out. Babe kept licking my tears, and I realize he's never done that before. When he did this in the past, he would lick a tear or two…and that was all. I took babe's head in my hands and looked very deep into his eyes. It was then that I could see that he was telling me to let him go. I said, "My Baby Boy…are you ready to go be with Jesus?" He blinked one time, and I knew he answered yes. Almost instantly, I had a peace about what I had to do.

There was no way that John was able to stay home, and I told him it was okay. To be honest, John cannot handle these situations very well nor can he even be in the room during the last moments with our dogs so it wouldn't have mattered to me. I certainly don't fault him for that. Some people can be there to the very end, and some people cannot.

John very tenderly said his goodbyes, and I sent him on his way. I wanted to be alone with Babe. It was so hard to believe that the time had come to let him go. In two more months, he would've been fifteen years old, and, like Frank, Babe lived past his life span by almost three years. He was always a good boy. I never had any problems with him. He was truly the best dog I've ever had.

I had to call a friend of mine to come over and help me get Babe into the back of my SUV where I laid with him while my friend drove to the animal hospital. I didn't want to put Babe through the stress of unloading him from the car and then help him, if I could into the hospital so I called Dr. H. on my way and asked her if he can go to sleep in my car. I would then transport him to the crematory myself, and she agreed. As hard as it was to say my final goodbyes to my Baby Boy, I still had a peace because he blinked at me one time.

I had Babe's cremains put into two containers, and I gave one of them to Anthony. After all, Babe was originally Anthony's dog.

I buried the other container in my backyard along with Frank and Breeze, under the big red rock, between the two palm trees. The three of them were the original Bowman Babies. They are locked in my heart forever and ever.

Chapter Twenty Four

PUMA

I am dedicating this chapter to my loving sister, Kathy, who went home to be with Jesus just one year ago today. We have suffered a great loss.

It seems that I can always find the good in all dogs and rescue the ones in need, and my sister always found the good in all people and she would rescue them. She even rescued a few animals too. If it weren't for Kathy, I don't know if this next rescue would have ever happened. Like my sister always said, "I can do all things through Christ who strengthens me" Philippians 4:13. I can even hear her voice. She proved this to be true to me on the day of this rescue. "Thank you Kathy. I love you and miss you."

After visiting Kathy at her house for the day, I was getting ready to leave, but we stopped in her driveway and talked a little bit longer when a pit bull came over to us waggin' her whole body and wearing that famous pit bull smile. Kathy said she had been roaming the neighborhood for several days. At that time, one of Kathy's neighbors came over to us asking if she was our dog.

Kathy said no and that nobody seemed to know where she lives. The neighbor said he has seen the dog approach children that were playing outside, and he was afraid she would bite one of the kids. He also said he would not hesitate shooting the dog.

That's when I spoke up and said, "Has she been aggressive to the kids?"

He said, "No, but you can't trust these kind of dogs."

So now I know I'm dealing with Mr. Ignorant and asked, "Are you talking about shooting a dog that has not hurt anybody nor showed any signs of hurting anybody?"

"I'll do what I have to do to protect my kids."

"Then you go ahead and protect your kids, and I'm going to protect this dog from ignorant people like you."

I turned to Kathy and told her this dog knew right where to go when she came to us and that I was taking her home.

The next day I made up some found flyers and took the dog and went back over to Kathy's neighborhood to post the flyers. I figured I'd walk the neighborhood with her to see if anybody knew her or where she lived. I no sooner got her out of my car on a leash when somebody yelled, "Hey, that's Candy, that's my dog."

My immediate thought was that I was glad I found her home, until I turned around and started walking towards the guy that said she was his dog. She clearly did not want to go to him. She had her tail tucked between her legs and crouched down low trying not to go any further. I didn't know what to do. I thought maybe I should just turn back around and start running away with her—or I should just throw her back in my car and take off. I really couldn't do anything. He already saw what I looked like and the car I drive…not to mention he lived right across the street from my sister Kathy.

I got mad and said, "If this is your dog, then you and I need to talk." I marched right up to him and said, "I saved your dog from being shot yesterday by one of your neighbors." I asked him why he lets her roam the neighborhood all the time.

He said she keeps escaping from the backyard to go play with the kids. Right then, I knew she was another lonely back yard dog who was just looking for attention.

I asked him if she is allowed to come in the house with him and his family. Of course he said no so I tried to explain to him that she is lonely. I told him to try and imagine himself having to stay in a backyard day after day, night after night, all alone, nobody to talk to, and nothing to do. I asked him how long he thought he'd be able to stand the loneliness. I also tried to explain to him how dangerous it is for her to be roaming the streets. She could get shot, run over by a car, attacked by another dog, attacked by a human or a punk kid. I didn't think I was getting anywhere with him and knew my hands were tied. Before I left, I told him to keep putting himself in her shoes and imagine how she must feel. The last thing I said was, "Please let her come in the house with the family. She just might want to stay home."

I asked Kathy to try and keep an eye on her, and if she sees her out of the back yard, to call me right away. I will take her home with me again—and she won't be back. I kept Kathy out of it as much as I could. He didn't even know that she was my sister. Every time I went to Kathy's, I looked for the dog but never saw it again. But, just a couple of months later, I spotted another little pit bull puppy in his back yard, all alone and crying. I was so upset and began crying for that baby who appeared to be just a few weeks old.

I told Kathy, "I've got to get that baby out of there." I just wasn't sure about how I was going to do it. My beautiful sister, being the faithful and obedient Christian that she is, said to me, "Connie, let's just pray for that baby right now." And, Kathy and I stood in her front yard, and we prayed hard for that baby.

Now this is where it gets really good…only two days later Kathy called me and said, "I was in my front yard watering and the little puppy from across the street walked right up to me." There IS power in prayer. She asked me what she should do. I told her to hold onto him and was on my way, but Kathy said not to come to her house because the people were not at home at that time. If they came home, she didn't want them to see me. She told me to meet her at her church, and I did. He was still in her van when I got there. When I opened the door to see him, he was so scared and shaking. I ran my hand down his back to comfort him, and he jumped right out of his skin. I told him it was okay, nobody was going to hurt him…and that he was safe, and his lonely days and nights were over. I thanked Jesus and thanked my sweet sister Kathy. I took the little guy home.

Kathy was so worried about me finding the right home for the little pup whom I named, "Puma." She's heard me talk about how hard it can be to find the best homes for these dogs, and on top of that, I do a very thorough screening process that sometimes could hinder an adoption.

There are never any guarantees to finding the best home, but all the more reason that I try to be thorough.

When I finally did find the best home for Puma, I called Kathy right away to tell her. She couldn't have been happier when I told her the home that I found for Puma was my own. I can't explain it, but I believe that this is where God wants Puma to be.

My sister, Sonya, always calls Kathy her, "Amazing Sister" and amazing…Kathy truly was.

Chapter Twenty Five

TENNIS SHOES

A friend of mine told me about some drug addicts that he knew who had two adult pit bulls that they bred and then had a litter of nine puppies.

Let me take a minute to share with you how I feel about breeding pit bulls, or any other kind of dog, or any other kind of animal, or any kind of human. I feel that nobody should be breeding anything. I don't care if you are a professional breeder, a backyard breeder, or a human breeder. The world is overpopulated with animals and people too. We domesticated some animals to benefit us in many ways, and WE are killing them by the millions every year because now, WE have too many of them. WE are taking away the natural habitats that the wild animals are living in because WE are overpopulated with people. God put animals on this land first, but WE are taking it away from them. Wild animals are being seen in communities more and more simply trying to survive on what they have left, and what do WE do? It's a wild animal. WE panic and WE kill it. I'm sure some people will have a different opinion, but this is mine.

My friend tells me that the dogs and the puppies are not being cared for, but I already knew that because just to breed the dog's shows irresponsibility to me. He said they are living in filth. Some of the puppies looked sick, but they were still trying to sell them. This did not come as a surprise either. I asked him if he would take me there, but he said no…he didn't want any trouble. I asked him why then was he even telling me about them.

"I thought that maybe you can buy one or two of them."

I asked him, 'Why would you think that? And, even if I could, what about the other puppies?"

He shrugged his shoulders.

With my own personal experience as a drug addict, all I can say is it takes one to know one.

I asked how much money did they want for the puppies. He said fifty dollars, or they would trade for dope. Again, my personal experience tells me that these people who have the puppies are straight out dope fiends. A dope fiend is just a different level of drug addiction. I still knew some connections so I spent fifty dollars for a half of a gram of Meth. I went to my friend and asked him again to take me there, but he refused. I gave him the half gram and told him to get me as many of the puppies that he could get. I also grabbed his arm as he turned to leave. I looked him straight in his eyes just like Frank used to do, and I said, "Don't be stupid and make me kick your ass."

He said, "I won't."

Before I let his arm go, I said, "If I can't kick your ass, I know somebody that can…and I will get some kicks in too."

"Okay."

I really didn't know anybody, but I had to get my point across. It always seemed to work for Frank.

A short time later, he brought me two puppies. I asked him about the other puppies, but he said, "These were the last two."

I don't know if I was happy or sad, but I knew that I didn't want to know any more about the puppies that I couldn't help anyway.

It then suddenly occurred to me that when Babe passed, that left me with just two dogs, Spot and Josephine. That was my promise to Breeze. I had finally reached my goal. "But wait, now you have Puma." Somehow I justified having three dogs again, and then—what seemed to be in the blink of an eye—I was back up to five.

What just happened here?

This is really not uncommon for people doing rescue work. In fact, if I am ever asked how many dogs I have, I always say, "Currently, I have…" but that number can change at any given moment or, even in the blink of an eye.

While trying to think of names for the two newbies, I decided to start my line of tennis shoes. I already had Puma so the newbies were named, "Nike and Fila." I even had a "Sketcher" at one time. Fila and Sketcher were adopted into loving homes, and like Puma, Nike became a Bowman.

One of the reasons why we kept Nike was because he became deathly ill twice. When doing rescue work, it is my responsibility to provide any and all medical treatments that are needed. Such as, spaying, neutering, vaccinating and micro chipping to name a few. This can be pretty expensive, and John and I are independent. Meaning we don't get donations or financial grants. We are not part of an organization, and we don't have volunteers. It is just John and I, and whatever is needed, comes out of our own pockets. Well, it mostly comes out of John's pockets.

In trying to save money, there was a local veterinarian giving discount vaccinations at a local feed store so that's where I took Nike. He needed three sets of puppy shots, four weeks apart. There was a very long line of people waiting with their pets to be vaccinated and

I applaud every one of them for being responsible pet owners. But, in spite of this, nobody knows if any of the dogs or puppies were already sick with diseases or viruses…and this could be an easy way for illnesses to spread. I might be wrong, but I believe that this is where Nike picked up the deadly Parvovirus. The day he got his third and final set of shots was the day I noticed he was sick. The very next day I took him to my regular doctor, and he tested positive for the virus that could kill a puppy within a couple of days.

Dr. G. said it would be very expensive ($1,000-$1,200) for treatment, but it is treatable. I talked it over with John, and we decided to go with the treatment. Dr. G. showed me how to do the I.V. treatment therapy so I could do it myself at home. Nike wouldn't have to be hospitalized which would cost even more money.

For the next three days, I felt like I was watching little Nike die slowly. I had never felt so helpless before in my life. I was doing everything Dr. G. told me to do, but he wasn't getting better. Seven days had passed by, and Nike had not eaten anything the entire seven days, not one crumb of anything. He was literally dying right before my eyes. And then, just as suddenly as he got sick, he suddenly started improving, and by the Grace of God, Nike made a full recovery. I made a full attachment to him having stayed by his side for every second that he was sick, hoping and praying that he would get better.

In less than one year later, I had to rush Nike to emergency. He had a high fever and was very lethargic. There was a decrease in his appetite and water intake. It turned out that he needed emergency surgery for a blockage in his lower intestine which could've killed him. This was estimated to cost another $1,200 which included a discount the doctor gave me because I worked in rescue. After the surgery, the doctor told us that he removed over a foot of what appeared to be shredded terry cloth and stuffing from a pillow or stuffed animal.

Once again, by the Grace of God, Nike made a full recovery. He is alive and well still to this day, and after almost $2,500, he is definitely a Bowman.

Chapter Twenty Six

BUDDY

There came a time for John and I to separate for reasons that were unrelated to rescuing. I decided that I should move out. I found a dog friendly apartment so I can bring my dogs over for sleepovers. The house was close so I could go over every day to spend time with them as well. But, when I brought Spot over and while we were out for a walk, I was approached by a security guard that said, "pit bulls are not allowed on this property and I advise you to get him off of the property now."

I told him, "Okay, we will leave now, I don't want any problems." But in my mind the words weren't quite the same. I knew of a time when this complex did in fact allow pit bulls and that's why I decided to move in there. I guess I should've been more specific when I asked if they still allowed dogs.

For me to not have a dog, left me feeling very lost and insecure. Starting when I was a little girl, I had become dependent on my dogs for a sense of security. If I thought I heard a scary noise, I would look at my dogs. If they were alert, I did hear a scary noise. If they were not alert, I knew it was all in my head.

For two weeks I was without a dog. Although, I went to the house every single day to be with my dogs, it was not the same as having a dog living with me. Sometimes, I would knock on some of my neighbor's doors and ask if I can pet their dogs, maybe take them for a walk. I'm sure, at first, they must have thought I was a crazy person.

I had been on an animal rescue network for animals in need and received an email about a twelve year old collie mix who was abandoned by his family and left tied to a tree for two weeks. Ironically, it was the same two weeks that I had been without a dog.

A Good Samaritan had been feeding and watering the dog thinking his owners were coming back…and then the dog stopped eating.

The dog's name was "Bud," and I knew I had to rescue him. He did not deserve to be left tied to a tree…and I needed a dog. I figured I can at least foster him until we find him a home. When I picked him up, my heart shattered once again. You could see the sadness and confusion in his eyes, and I knew his heart had been shattered too.

I took him to my apartment and made him a nice fluffy bed and filled a food and water bowl for him. I offered him some treats, but he didn't want them. He went to his bed and laid down so I left the treats right by his bed for when he wanted them. I sat next to his bed and tried to comfort him the best that I could. He was a lost soul. He didn't understand, and neither did I.

I hated the people he used to belong to for what they did to him. He loved them unconditionally for twelve long years, loyal to the end—and they tied him to a tree and abandoned him.

For the following three weeks, my heart broke more and more each day for Bud. He was not getting better. He was grieving for his family, and I thought his grief was going to kill him. He wouldn't eat and drank very little water. Nothing seemed to make him happy, but I kept trying. We'd go on several walks every day. I'd groom him and tell him how beautiful he was. I'd pet him and tell him that I was sorry he was hurting, that I wished I could take his pain away. I prayed that God would take his pain away, and sometimes I'd just sit with him and not say anything. I felt his pain, and he was in a lot of it.

If we weren't outside walking, he would be laying in his bed with his head down…and that's where he stayed until the next walk. I had to go to work. It was so hard to leave him, but thankfully, I was only working six hours a day. As soon as I got off work, I'd rush right home because I didn't want him to be alone any more than he had to be. When I got home, I'd find him lying in his bed. He didn't greet me at the door when I came in, he didn't wag his tail happy to see me, and he never even acknowledged that I was there. I'd take him for a walk, and he'd go right back to his bed.

I was so worried about him. I truly thought he was going to die grieving for his family. Then, after three long weeks, I rushed home from work and when I opened the door, Bud was right there wagging his tail, just a little, but enough to let me know that he was happy to see me. And every day after that, when I'd get home from work and opened the door, there was Bud.

I had been so focused on Bud and his happiness that I completely forgot about my unhappiness due to John and me separating…Bud had rescued me too. There is no doubt in my mind that God wanted Bud and I to be together…to rescue each other.

John and I got back together, even re-married. I moved back home and brought Bud with me. He is now a Bowman. Although he is now fourteen years old, can barely see and hardly hear, he has remained happy ever since that one day that I opened the door and found him there, wagging his tail for the first time. Praise God.

Chapter Twenty Seven

WALLY & PATRICK

My best friend's son called me one day and told me he had just witnessed some punk kids throw a pit bull puppy over a five foot wall. He and his friends ran to check on the puppy which they had with them when they called me. I told him to hold on to her, that John and I were on our way.

When we got there and I checked out the puppy, she appeared to be okay, although she was terribly shaking. The kids told me that they knew where the punk kids lived so I went to pay them a visit—but of course nobody answered the door. I decided to take the pup to the vet to make sure that she was in fact okay. I'd go back to the house later. The vet said there were no broken bones, and she was just shook up pretty good but should be fine in a couple of days.

I took her to my house and got her settled. I then went back to where the punks lived, and again, nobody answered so I reported the incident to the police and to animal control. What happened after that, I have no clue. This is just one case that was brought to my attention that involved kids and animal cruelty. It makes me sick to my stomach to think of how many more cases like this exist that nobody even knows about. It reminds me of a very long time ago when I saw three kids chasing a bunny rabbit with sticks and rocks. When I realized what they were doing, I picked up the biggest stick I could find, which was more like a tree branch, and I started chasing them until they disappeared. Nothing was ever done to these kids nor, to the kids that threw the puppy over the wall.

I placed a found ad with her picture and said that she had been thrown over a wall. Normally, I don't put pictures on a found ad because I want the person to describe to me the animal that they lost to ensure the animal goes back to its rightful owner. Nobody called to claim her. She was a very sweet little girl whom I affectionately started calling, "Wally."

In less than a week, I got another call asking for my help. The caller said she was at a busy intersection when she saw a dog run right through the intersection like a bat out of hell.

She followed him to try to help him. When she pulled over to get out of her car, he jumped right in. She said his eyes were as big as half dollars, and he was shaking uncontrollably. She took him to her house and thought she'd keep him in her garage until she could figure out what to do. When she parked her car in the garage and shut the garage door, she then couldn't get the dog out of her car.

I wanted to go there right away, but I had to stop and think for a minute, for a change. I just brought Wally into my house which brought me up to six dogs, and legally, I am only licensed to have up to six dogs. "Okay, so I won't be bringing this one home, but I could at least go over to see what I could do, if anything."

When I got there, the first thing she told me was that her husband would absolutely flip out if he knew she had a stray in her garage.

She said, "I think if it's a pit bull, it will make it even worse."

I heard what she said, but I was more concerned about the dog itself, no matter what it was.

It was a pit bull, and he still had fear in his eyes and was shaking uncontrollably. He was not getting out of the car. She had put some blankets in the car for him, and he had buried himself in them so I couldn't see his body. She said he was very skinny. It was apparent that something or somebody had him scared to death, and it was breaking my heart. I sat with him for a while and just talked to him, I told him it was okay and promised I wasn't going to hurt him—and neither would anybody else. He just shook. I slowly reached out to him. He shook more. I knew then that this poor boy had been abused. I asked the lady if she could get me some lunch meat. I offered it to him, and he shook even harder, but I think the hunger pains got the best of him and he took a bite. Little by little and inch by inch, I lead him out of the car with the lunch meat. When I could finally see his whole body, my heart then busted. I had to keep feeding him. I had to gain his trust. He appeared to be approximately a year old but was extremely emaciated. He had bite wounds on his forelegs and around his head and face. His nails were so long, it surprised me he could even stand. This indicated to me that he had not been on the run for long or they would've been worn down. Considering this and the fearful state he was in, I believed that this poor baby had just escaped his abuser. I also thought that this poor baby was kept in a car, and it was his comfort zone...and that's why he didn't want to get out of the car that he jumped into.

We put blankets on the floor. I sat with him and kept feeding him and talking to him. I started to feel a little panic coming on because I know I have to take this baby. I asked the lady if she could keep him for just a little while until I could figure out something else. As if he heard me, the husband opens the door, and just like she said, he flipped out. The poor dog ran right back to the car.

"Get that f-ing pit bull out of here now," he yelled.

I told him that I was trying to figure it out and promised I will get him out of there. I was crying. I begged and pleaded with him to just give me a little time, just a couple of hours.

"I'll take him away, I promise."

To my surprise he said, "You have one hour."

I immediately had to try to comfort the dog again. I'm thinking...I have too many dogs at my house already, I have no available resources. I had to figure something out, and I couldn't even think clearly. I was not leaving this baby there, no way. I managed to get him into my car, and we left. I was crying so hard out of anger that I couldn't even see to drive, and I had to pull over so I could get a hold of my emotions. I looked at this terrified dog still wide eyed and shaking. I thought to myself that I just can't do this anymore, but I screamed, "Please God...help me save this baby."

I took him home, set him up in my office, and made him as comfortable as I could. He was still shaking and very tense. Like I do with all of my sick or injured dogs, I cooked my special recipe and hand fed him which helped me to slowly gain his trust. I had to remember to move slowly around him and try to keep things quiet because he spooked at everything. He was full of fear and completely exhausted. I cannot imagine what he had been through. I praised God that he was safe now. I named him, "Patrick."

I took him to my vet to be examined. Dr. B. said that he was about a year old, and he should've weighed around forty to forty five pounds. Patrick weighed only twenty eight pounds. I decided to wait to have him neutered because he was too physically and mentally fragile. Anything or any sounds that were unfamiliar to him, which was pretty much everything, he would jump right out of his own skin. Several times a day, I had to hand feed him small portions of my special recipe so he wouldn't get sick. He always ate so fast and never left a crumb. When I stopped hand feeding him and he was eating out of a bowl, he would lick his bowl clean; and then one day, a day I will always remember, he walked away with food still in his bowl. He had finally had his fill.

My focus was on Patrick and his well-being. I'm sure my other dogs felt a little neglected, but I knew that they still had John. Up until I brought Patrick home, he didn't have anybody. To let them know that I still loved them, I gave them my recipe too.

I slept in the office with Patrick for the first week or so, but he kept a distance between us, until one morning when I woke up and he was lying right next to me. That was exactly what I was waiting for, for him to come to me. I gave him time and gave him his space—and he gave me his trust and his heart. He was still very timid, but I knew he was coming out of his shell.

Patrick and I were getting very close, but he was very uneasy around John, around men in general. John understood and gave him his space, and after a short while, I could tell that Patrick was trying and wanted to trust John.

Patrick had already been with Wally, and the two of them got along really good. He didn't show any signs of aggression towards the other dogs when he would see them through the office doors. He showed a lot of interest, and since Bobo was the most laid back and easygoing, I let him and Patrick meet first. It went well so I let him meet Josie and then Nike and then Puma. He did good with them too. Because Spot and Bud were in their senior years, I thought it would be best to just leave the two of them as they were. I kept them separated from the other dogs that were all closer in age. But then, I noticed that Patrick would growl whenever he saw Bud—and I couldn't figure out why. He never growled at any of the other dogs, just Bud. Sometimes I would be in the office with just Patrick. I then noticed that if any of the dogs would walked past the office doors, he started growling at them too. It appeared to me that he felt that he had to protect me. I wondered what was going on with him because he was doing so well. I hoped that I wasn't going to start having problems with Patrick, but I did.

I had to pay close attention to him, and in doing so, I could see that something was triggering Patrick. It looked like he was having flashbacks…like the time when Bobo, Patrick, and I were taking a nap one afternoon. I was still awake when suddenly, Patrick woke up out of a dead sleep and tried to attack Bobo. Thank God I was there, and Bobo was on the other side of me because when I sat up, I blocked Patrick. I yelled, "Patrick" and he snapped out of it. Whatever "it" was, John was able to gain Patrick's trust, but every now and then, Patrick would have a setback and become very fearful again. It had become clear to me that I couldn't trust him; however, I understood. I knew that his behavior came out of his past history. Most of the time he was very sweet and loving, even comical, and I still loved him.

I knew that I wouldn't be able to put Patrick up for adoption. I take pride in being a responsible and respectful rescuer. I cannot adopt out an unpredictable dog. Unless it was the dog whisperer himself that wanted to adopt Patrick, and even then, I would be apprehensive. After talking to John about this dilemma, we decided that we had no other choice but to keep him.

I was one dog over my legal limit which could've jeopardized them all so I had Wally fully vetted and then went to work hard on getting her adopted. A couple weeks later, she found her forever home.

I was back down to six dogs, but I have to admit there was no difference in having six dogs or seven dogs.

Patrick had developed the cutest personality and brought me so much joy when he wasn't in a triggered state of mind. He made me laugh every day. I was very attached to him, but I worried about him and his flashbacks. I worried about if I was going to be able to handle him properly. I wasn't afraid that he would hurt me although his flashbacks were pretty scary. I also had to worry about John and the other dogs, I was not sure if he would try to hurt them. I prayed that would never happen, and I prayed for healing of his mental state of mind. I had to stay alert and on my toes.

I had to have the cable company come to the house one day. The tension was high with six dogs all paired up and behind closed doors. There was still barking and whining and crying because a stranger was in the house. Patrick and Josie were in the office where they could clearly see the cable guy. Josie wasn't barking much, but Patrick was. While I was trying to talk over all the barking, I turned towards Patrick and Josie and said, "Quiet." Patrick was acting aggressively at the door and then re-directed his aggression towards Josie. I almost panicked but told the cable guy to quickly step outside. I quickly got Josie out of the office unhurt. Patrick didn't bite her at all. Unfortunately the cable guy was not finished with his work so I put Josie in another room.

The cable guy had already been there for over an hour and I was stressed out to the max. The barking continued, and I just couldn't take it anymore. I yelled out again, "Quiet," throwing out my arms at the same time and not realizing that I was holding a towel in my hand. When I threw out my arms, they went towards Patrick. The gesture triggered Patrick, who then bared his teeth snarling, and he charged at me. I thank God the office doors were closed and between us because I believe he would've hurt me. I regret to say that Patrick was a ticking time bomb.

The cable guy finally left. The dogs finally calmed down, but there was still tension in the air. I was having a hard time calming myself down and just sat in a stupor thinking about the two very close calls that I just had—and how everybody and the dogs were not safe with Patrick in the house. Sadly, deep down I knew what I had to do, but I think I was in denial about it. I told myself that there has to be other options…"I have to save Patrick's life."

For the next two weeks or so, I was desperately seeking an

alternative from Patrick going to sleep. I blamed myself for what happened the day he charged at me. It was a very stressful day, more stress than he could handle. The gesture I made with my arms happened to go in his direction and the towel in my hand made him feel threatened. I shouldn't have had him in the office where he could see the cable guy. I came up with many more excuses for why he charged at me. I didn't blame Patrick at all. But at the same time, I knew that I did not have the experience needed to have a dog that was so traumatized and unpredictable.

I was apprehensive about going into the same room with him, but when things had calmed down that day, I looked at Patrick. I knew he wasn't in that aggressive mode any more. There was a look in his eyes that said he was no longer a threat to me so I went into the office with him. He was back to being himself, sweet and loving and goofy and comical…like nothing ever even happened.

I sent out pleas to everybody I knew or had experience with traumatized dogs. I posted pleas on the social networks asking for advice, suggestions, and directions. I was begging for any kind of help I could get. I emailed three different Veterinarians that I had worked for and trusted, explaining everything I knew about Patrick and his behavior. I was hoping and praying for another option. But, every response that came back to me was the same: the only responsible thing to do would be to humanely euthanize Patrick.

I had to convince myself that I gave it my best shot, and I failed. I had to give Patrick to God. It kills me to think that whoever did this to Patrick is probably still alive and well.

I am grateful for the few months that I had to love Patrick. I buried his cremains with the others, under the big red rock, in between the two palm trees. I will hold him in my heart forever as well. He too was a Bowman.

Chapter Twenty Eight

OVER THE RAINBOW

When it comes to the dogs, I am more like the disciplinarian, and John is the softy. What I would call a dogs "bad manners," John would call cute. John also has a hard time resisting their begging eyes. When he thinks I'm not looking, he'll slip the dogs something to eat that I would prefer them not to have, or he'll give them more cookies then they should have. Because I am so adamant about keeping their weight at the norm, I rarely will give them cookies.

Josie, Bobo, Nike, and Puma were all putting the weight on so instead of buying the large size dog biscuits, we started buying the medium size to help with their weight management. After a few months, they started looking slimmer. And then, it seemed like overnight, Bobo dropped a lot of weight. I knew that it was not normal, but when my Bobo refused a carrot, which was his all-time favorite, I knew something was wrong. I took him to one of my vets.

Dr. L. wanted to keep Bobo for a couple of hours to run some tests and told me he'd call me when I could pick him up. But, when Dr. L. called, he had devastating news. He said that he found a very large and very aggressive tumor in Bobo's abdomen. It felt like a horse had just kicked me in the head. I knew my Bo wasn't well, but I never anticipated this. Bobo was three years old, but Dr. L. said he had to be much older because of the size and aggression of the tumor he found in Bobo, was typically found in much older dogs. I told Dr. L. that he was still a baby when I rescued him three years before.

"Does that mean that the tumor has been there for a long time, and I never noticed it?"

Was "Guilty" written on my forehead?

How could I have missed this?

The doctor said that there was no way I could've known. I then remembered one day when Bobo was in the backyard and I came out with Patrick. I watched Patrick go over to play with Bo, but then stopped and sniffed his belly. He then kind of turned his nose and walked away from Bobo. I was puzzled about Patrick's actions, and I thought, "That was peculiar." Partick knew.

Dr. L. said that we could try this test or that test, but there were no guarantees because the tumor was very aggressive. I called John. He met me at the hospital and together we talked to the doctor. We then decided to let Bobo cross over The Rainbow Bridge. I didn't even get to bring my Bo back home. When I did bring him home, he was in an urn which I buried under the big red rock between the two palm trees and forever in my heart.

Just yesterday, I received some devastating news about Spot. I noticed an oblong shaped lump on his back leg. With him pushing fourteen years, I didn't waste any time getting him to my vet. I feared the worst. I feared cancer. Spot is a pit bull / Boxer mix, and I knew that Boxers are prone to cancer. Dr. B. said right away that it was Spot's lymph nodes and suggested that he aspirate the lump so he could know more. I had to wait five long days for the results. Dr. B. said that it was cancer. Somehow, I already knew it was.

I really don't know how to explain it, and I don't even know why, but for a long time I knew that Spot had cancer; maybe it was my intuition. When Bobo was diagnosed with cancer, I thought that I just got the dogs mixed up, and it wasn't Spot that had cancer after all. Turns out, I was right the first time.

Once again, I was faced with making that dreaded decision. I had to carefully consider Spot's age, close to fourteen years old. He couldn't hear very well anymore, had cataracts in his eyes, and couldn't see very well anymore. This caused him to have a lot of anxiety. Many times he misjudged jumping on the bed—and he'd miss. I didn't want to put him through a series of tests and trials that wasn't going to make him better. Although he wasn't suffering, I didn't want to wait until he was. So in my heart, I knew that the last, but the best thing for me to do for Spot was to let him go over The Rainbow Bridge to be with Jesus where I know the others are as well. But, how do I decide what day it will be? Today? Maybe tomorrow?

I remember the very first time I saw Spot, he was a mess; but, like Red and so many others, I instantly fell in love with him the very second I laid my eyes on him. I knew I had to have him. Sonya and I signed the adoption papers for Spot and Connor the same day. I can remember how proud I was that Spot was officially mine. In spite of his ears being cut off and the bite scars that he wore, he was a beautiful dog inside and out, all white with one large brown spot over his left eye…hence, the name Spot. He was an ambassador for the bully breeds with a personality that could prove to the coldest of hearts that bullies are certainly worth saving and loving.

I can only speculate on his misery in his first year of life. I know in the thirteen years that followed, I tried to give him my best, and without a doubt, I did give him my heart…and in return, he gave me his too.

Can I let him go today? I don't think I can. Am I being selfish and trying to hang on? I think I am.

Sadly, while I am trying to hang onto Spot, Buddy starts having a few seizures. He is no longer steady on his feet and sometimes falls down. Buddy no longer sleeps through the night; instead, he paces and wanders aimlessly or just circles. He gets stuck in corners and seems disorientated by standing at the hinge side of a door. He leaks urine, his vision is clouded by cataracts, and his hearing has diminished. To get his attention, I have to clap my hands, and then he looks at me and doesn't know who I am. Buddy is fourteen.

I cannot believe that I am faced with making that dreaded decision for not only one of my beloved dogs but now two. Lately, I feel like all I've been doing is deciding who is going to die and when. It seems ironic considering I rescued these dogs to save their lives.

Spot and Buddy crossed over The Rainbow Bridge. I will bring home their cremains as well, and they will be buried with the others under the big red rock in between the two palm trees and in my heart forever and ever.

There's a lot of heartache that goes with rescuing. I hope and pray that my work was done well, and my dogs knew joy and happiness and how much I truly loved…and still love every one of them. I pray that they all know that I loved them enough…to let them go.

In rescuing, there are also rewards. To simply be able to love a rescued dog and feel their love in return, and to see the gratitude in their eyes, is a reward like no other. To nurture them out of their shells and see the tension in their bodies melt away as you gain their trust. To see their tails wag for the first time, to watch them learn how to play and learn new sights and smells. These are all rewards in rescuing, and there are many more.

Knowing that, along with all the heartache, there are many more rewards, and I will continue to rescue my beloved bullies and others, till the day I die. It is my calling. It is my duty. It is the reason The Good Lord put me on this earth.

"I rescue animals...my work is never done, my home is never quiet, my wallet is always empty, but my heart is always full." ~ Annette King–Tucker ~

THE RESCUER'S LAST REWARD

Unlike most days at the Rainbow Bridge, this day dawned cold and gray. All the recent arrivals at the Bridge did not know what to think, as they had never seen such a day. But the animals who had been waiting longer for their beloved people to accompany them across the Bridge knew what was happening, and they began to gather at the pathway leading to the Bridge.

Soon an elderly dog came into view, head hung low and tail dragging. He approached slowly—and though he showed no sign of injury or illness—he was in great emotional pain. Unlike the animals gathered along the pathway, he had not been restored to youth and vigor upon arriving at the Bridge. He felt out of place and wanted only to cross over and find happiness. But as he approached the Bridge, his way was barred by an angel, who apologized and explained that the tired and broken-spirited old dog could not cross over. Only those animals accompanied by their people were allowed to cross the Bridge.

Having nobody, and with nowhere else to turn, the dog trudged into the field in front of the Bridge. There he found others like himself, elderly or infirm, sad and discouraged. Unlike the other animals waiting to cross the Bridge, these animals were not running or playing. They simply were lying in the grass, staring forlornly at the pathway across the Rainbow Bridge. The old dog took his place among them, watching the pathway and waiting—yet not knowing for what he was waiting.

One of the newer dogs at the Bridge asked a cat, who had been there longer, to explain what was happening. The cat replied, "Those poor animals were abandoned, turned away, or left at rescue places, but they never found a home on earth. They all passed on with only the love of a rescuer to comfort them. Because they had no people to love them, they have nobody to escort them across the Rainbow Bridge."

The dog asked the cat, "So what will happen to those animals?" Before the cat could answer, the clouds began to part, and the cold turned to bright sunshine. The cat replied, "Watch, and you will see."

In the distance was a single person. As he approached the Bridge, the old, infirm and sad animals in the field were bathed in a golden light. They were at once made young and healthy, and they stood to see what their fate would be. The animals, who had previously gathered at the pathway, bowed their heads as the person approached. At each bowed head, the person offered a scratch or hug. One by one, the now youthful and healthy animals from the field fell into line behind the person. Together, they walked across the Rainbow Bridge to a future of happiness and unquestioned love.

The dog asked the cat, "What just happened?"

The cat responded, "That was a rescuer. The animals gathered along the pathway bowing in respect were those who had found their forever homes because of rescuers. They will cross over when their people arrive at the Bridge. The arrival here of a rescuer is a great and solemn event, and as a tribute, they are permitted to perform one final act of rescue. They are allowed to escort all those poor animals they couldn't place on earth across the Rainbow Bridge."

The dog thought for a moment, then said, "I like rescuers."

The cat smiled and replied, "So does heaven, my friend. So does heaven."

~~ Unknown ~~

"You Made Me"

You made me what I am today, courage at its best.
You wanted me to know no fear, a cut above the rest.
Not only did I master that, I've thrown in loyalty, too.
Look past my eyes into my soul, you know I'd die for you.
I'll watch your kids, I'll watch your house.
Your praise will be my crown,
Ask what you will—I'll do my best.
I'll even be your clown.
But some of you don't like me, I'm sure I don't know why.
The only thing I'm guilty of is courage, love, and try.
But still they want to see me go, they want my breed to end.
Will I see you sitting idly by? You, whom I call a friend?
You made me what I am today, you never saw me waiver.
I've done my best to keep you safe.
Won't you please return the favor?

~~ Unknown ~~

IN HONOR OF...

Frank

Trooper

Babe

Helen

Breeze

Daney

Spot

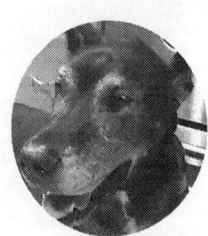

Connor

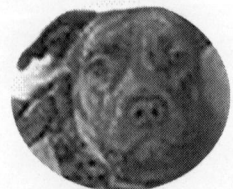

Honey

Bug

IN HONOR OF...

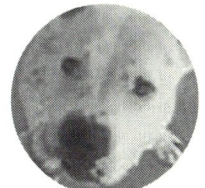
Josie

Patrick

Baby Boy

Wally

Candy

Buddy

Puma

Ellen

Nike

Roadie

Pinto
Red
Boss
Boogie
Bobo
Fila
Sketcher
Moses
Mesa
Bruno
K.O.
Grizzly
Sweetie
Shorty
Sable
Noble
Cheyenne
Craig
Paco
Roxy
Chowder
Hazelnut
Facho
Puddles
Miss Bossy

For More Information, visit

ConnieToTheRescue.com

Made in the USA
Charleston, SC
04 December 2013

125 ESSAYS

N. CANAGARATHNAM
R.N.B.Sc (Nsg), DIP. in Management
SP.Psy.Nsg.Tr, Certified Counsellor
Chief Special Grade Nursing Officer
Teaching Hospital,
Jaffna, Sri Lanka.